7/12/11
#34.95

CONSPIRACY RISING

CONSPIRACY RISING

Conspiracy Thinking and American Public Life

Martha F. Lee

 PRAEGER

AN IMPRINT OF ABC-CLIO, LLC
Santa Barbara, California • Denver, Colorado • Oxford, England

Every reasonable effort has been made to trace the owners of copyright materials in this book, but in some instances this has proven impossible. The author and publisher will be glad to receive information leading to more complete acknowledgments in subsequent printings of the book and in the meantime extend their apologies for any omissions.

Library of Congress Cataloging-in-Publication Data

Lee, Martha F. (Martha Frances), 1962–
   Conspiracy rising : conspiracy thinking and American public life / Martha F. Lee.
      p. cm.
   Includes bibliographical references and index.
   ISBN 978-0-313-35013-9 (alk. paper) — ISBN 978-0-313-35014-6 (ebook)
   1. Conspiracies—United States.   2. United States—Civilization—1970– —Psychological aspects.   I. Title.
   E169.12.L395   2011
   973.924—dc22   2011008496

ISBN: 978-0-313-35013-9
EISBN: 978-0-313-35014-6

15   14   13   12   11   1   2   3   4   5

This book is also available on the World Wide Web as an eBook.
Visit www.abc-clio.com for details.

Praeger
An Imprint of ABC-CLIO, LLC

ABC-CLIO, LLC
130 Cremona Drive, P.O. Box 1911
Santa Barbara, California 93116-1911

This book is printed on acid-free paper ∞

Manufactured in the United States of America

For Iain

"Everyone loves a conspiracy."

—Dan Brown, *The Da Vinci Code*

Contents

Introduction

An evil group of men has always wanted to rule the entire world. In the past conquest has failed to achieve this, due to the resulting outrage and awareness of the enemy. In our present time an evil group are trying a subtle but effective way to rule. This is to gradually infiltrate and delude the masses into accepting their ideas. Such subtle gradualism, along with distraction (such as unnecessary work, study, entertainment and sport) is being used effectively. Few people will therefore be aware of what is going on.[1]

—Richard Hole, "True Conspiracies"

Today, talk of conspiracy pervades water-cooler discussions, Internet sites, and popular entertainment. Conspiracy theories exist that purport to explain matters as trivial as sports and entertainment, as well as some of the most significant economic and political issues of our times. Websites warn us that if any NFL game seems "too good to be true," it is because the game has been fixed;[2] that Paul McCartney's death in a 1966 car crash means that a look-alike has replaced him for the past 45 years;[3] and that perhaps the notion that we need to drink eight glasses of water per day is a fabrication to encourage us to drink bottled water.[4] More significantly, conspiracy theories have also come to pervade our political lives.

Some of the most significant of these conspiracy theories challenge political legitimacy and therefore have a potentially serious impact on the health of democratic political regimes. The American "Birther" movement, for example, claims—despite thorough evidence to the contrary—that Barack Obama is not an American citizen, and therefore ineligible to serve as president of the United States. The circulation of these types of theories has a political impact. A CNN poll in July of 2010 found that only 42 percent of Americans were certain that Obama was born in the United States.[5]

Whether or not you are a believer or a skeptic, it is difficult to escape discussions of conspiracy. They are everywhere. For believers, the prevalence
of conspiratorial warnings is evidence of the veracity of their beliefs. We are
living in special times. It is up to us to act now to prevent the conspirators
from coming to power and preserve what is left of our liberty. In what we
are told is the most important battle in human history, it is we and our era
that are most critical. From warnings that a secret group of Jewish bankers
is plotting a New World Order, to arguments that Barack Obama is in league
with the Illuminati, and his presidency the final stage in installing totalitarian socialism in America, conspiracy theorists tell us that it is we and our
times that are decisive. Can this be? Are we all that stands between life as we
know it and an apocalyptic hell? If so, we had better join in the fight.

Those less inclined to accept a conspiratorial worldview are likely to scoff
at such dire warnings, and even mock those who believe them.[6] The "Glenn
Beck Conspiracy Theory Generator," for example, promises "Fair and Bal-
anced Paranoia, Delivered on Demand."[7] Using common conspiracy villains, themes, and goals, along with various slogans of the political right and
other miscellaneous terms, it generates slightly skewed conspiracy theories
that fit surprisingly well into the conspiracy oeuvre. One such theory, for
example, warns, "There are crypto-Muslim sleeper agents in every part of
the government who are releasing flying monkeys as we speak to help them
enslave you in FEMA camps."[8] Similarly, a wide variety of blogs criticize
Hillary Clinton's use of conspiracy theory to defend herself.[9] Criticisms of
Clinton's claims are almost as prevalent on the right, as are the conspiracy
theories of the left. Indeed, Clinton's claims are also sometimes used for co-
medic effect. In 2008, for example, in attempting to explain some unusual
behavior, Alec Baldwin complained that he had been the victim of a "vast
right-wing conspiracy."[10] Many nonbelievers' responses suggest that they
view such beliefs as a subject for humor rather than as politically significant
in any way.

This book challenges both conspiratorial ideas and those who dis-
miss them as trivial. Instead, it considers conspiratorial belief systems as
inherently meaningful, not as true assessments of reality, but instead, as
representations of a community's experiences and concerns. In their architecture, choice of conspiratorial villains and victims, and in their view
of the world's future, these theories can tell us much about the nature of
political life. Fundamentally, conspiracy theories concern political power,
and their popularity during particular periods of human history is related

to shifts in the distribution of power, both within states, and in their international relations. Conspiracy theories therefore deserve reasonable and serious political analysis because they provide insight into how believers perceive the ways in which political power is used, and because these perceptions can influence their actions.

The book begins with an analysis of conspiracy thinking and a consideration of its different forms. There is an important distinction to be made regarding the ways in which the dominant conspiracy discourse has changed in the last 100 years. Discussions of conspiracy once focused on specific political events, for example, the assassination of John F. Kennedy or the death of Elvis Presley, and while these have continued, today we are perhaps more likely to hear that a conspiracy exists that is working to dominate every aspect of our existence. Typically these "superconspiracies" involve a number of secret groups, working in concert, and include such villains as the Illuminati, Freemasons, or Knights Templar. Some of the most popular conspiracy theories today, those which concern the New World Order and/ or the North American Union, are of this type. The Illuminati, Freemasons, and Templars figure prominently in these efforts. There are good reasons why these groups are selected as the evil powers working to control the world. A consideration of the documented history of the Big Three conspiratorial villains provides insights into the reasons why they are often selected as the secret controlling forces of world history.

How did superconspiracies become such a popular way of understanding economics and politics? Interestingly, the person most responsible for this transformation of conspiracy thinking is Nesta Webster, a British woman who developed her theories in the first half of the 20th century. Webster was convinced that the world's secret societies worked in concert, aiming to destroy British civilization. Her ideas found a significant audience during her lifetime; her books went into multiple editions, and she became a right-wing celebrity, running her own political information center in central London.

The majority of Webster's books remain in print today, and her influence can be found particularly in the conspiracy theories of the American far right (including the Militia and Patriot movements). Webster's life and ideas are discussed in chapter 3, and they suggest an important theme of this book. The nature of the economic, social, and political upheaval of Webster's lifetime conditioned her vision of a world torn by an intense and ultimate conflict between evil conspirators and their victims, a battle brought to a head by Britain's loss of hegemony, and the forces of globalization. In a world where it was becoming increasingly obvious that events in one state could affect others, conspiracy discourse accommodated that new reality by expanding the number of its villains, and the scope of their reach.

This argument is considered in more detail in chapter 4, which examines what international relations scholars call "long cycles" of global politics. At the conclusion of each long cycle, a period during which the hegemonic power of the era is declining in its ability to maintain order in the international system, there appears to be a spike in the popularity of conspiracy theory. As the United Provinces declined, conspiracy theory first emerged as a mode of political explanation. As Britain began to lose its capacity to dominate the world system, conspiracy theory became a popular form of discourse once more, and in the new globalized world, appeared in a new globalized form. As the United States' capacity to order the international system has declined, conspiracy theory has become a powerful force in American politics.

The events of September 11, 2001, were a stark and tragic reminder that in the 21st-century world, political will could be violently expressed internationally, in unexpected ways. Relying on an airport security network that had perhaps grown complacent, and Western expectations that terrorists would want to preserve their own lives, 19 hijackers used American airliners, in American cities, to strike at symbols of American global power: the World Trade Center and the Pentagon. Passengers ensured that the third airplane—likely aimed at another Washington target, the Capitol or the White House—would not reach its target. They forced it into a Pennsylvania field. In scope and power these actions had no precedent, and for a nation historically protected from such violence by its geography and military power, they were shocking.

Almost immediately, the search for explanations began, and for many, the only rationale could possibly be that the government must have known in advance of the attacks, and perhaps was even responsible for them. For others, the attack was one component of a Zionist plot to control the world. "Didn't you know," said one of my students about a week later, "that 4,000 Jews didn't show for work at the World Trade Center on September 11?" He was not alone in this outrageous belief; the idea that a secret network had informed its allies of the impending disaster still circulates on the Internet. Chapter 5 considers why, in the wake of such a human tragedy, so many people, including thousands of Americans, would conclude that the

U.S. government, and/or a religious minority, would wish to kill innocent citizens.

The prevalence of conspiracy theory as a mode of political discourse during particular historical periods suggests that it is a response to uncertain conditions. Chapter 6 makes clear that there are particular dangers inherent in its structure. Conspiracy theory fosters two paradoxical tendencies: apathy and political extremism. Both of these propensities are unhealthy for the political community. Conspiracy thinking encourages believers to view the political world in a dualistic frame. It emphasizes a distinction between "us" and "them," and therefore promotes a hostile political environment. Opponents become enemies. Politics, however, is not just about speech, it is also about action. For this reason, conspiracy theories can also be used to justify violence. While political apathy may not seem to be as great a threat, within democracies it too is problematic. If citizens are not vigilant and/or choose not to participate in the democratic process, government may overstep its limits and violate their rights and freedoms. By their very belief that the world is dominated by a conspiracy bent on destroying their freedom, conspiracy believers may in fact play a vital role in allowing their government to engage in just such a violation.

This project began in the Cambridge University Library, where I came across Nesta Webster's many books, and was moved by her life story to pursue the question that has driven this research: why do people choose to believe in conspiracy theories? In beginning to answer that query, this research was supported by a grant from the Social Sciences and Humanities Research Council of Canada, and a fellowship at Clare Hall, University of Cambridge. As the project expanded, it was furthered by my tenure as the Stephen Jarislowsky Chair in Religion and Conflict, a position which provided the necessary time and resources to complete this work. Over the course of this project, I have also had the assistance of a number of graduate research students; Jennifer Jannuska, Craig Brannagan, Jack MacClennan, and Herb Simms are deserving of special mention. I am also indebted to Paul Green, whose redrawing of Nesta Webster's Chart of the World Revolution artfully clarifies her arguments. Any errors or omissions in this book are my own responsibility.

For many reasons, this project took a number of years to come to fruition. I owe a great debt to many people, including a very patient editor and colleagues who tolerated my intellectual meanderings on this topic. Thanks are also due to my friends and extended family, who were similarly long-suffering.

I am most grateful, however, for the support of my immediate family, who endured far too many dinner-table discussions concerning conspiracy theories and politics than anyone should have to, and did so with great patience. In this as in all else, I am indebted to John Sutcliffe, whose kindness, generosity, and sense of humor help me find joy every day, and to Rory and Iain, who question everything, and know that our world is one of infinite possibilities.

Chapter 1

I Want to Believe

The Al Qaeda attacks of September 11, 2001, transformed American politics; they changed the federal government's domestic and international policy agendas, individual citizens' sense of identity and security, and even the nation's conception of itself and its place in the world. The Global Language Monitor, an organization that analyzes and tracks language usage, notes that 9/11 also changed American political discourse. New words and phrases, such as "Ground Zero," entered the lexicon. Notably, too, the tone of political discussion became increasingly vitriolic. Opponents were openly called liars and even compared to Fascists. The Monitor comments that it is as if, "in the face of a nearly invisible, constantly morphing, enemy, we have turned the attack inward, upon ourselves, and our institutions."[1] As Americans and the world came to terms with the events of September 11, a significant minority questioned the government's account of that day. Among the alternative explanations that appeared was the assertion that it was in fact the U.S. government itself that had initiated an attack on its own citizens. In a 2006 Scripps Howard poll, 36 percent of those surveyed stated that they believed the American government participated in the attacks or knew about them, and did nothing to stop their occurrence.[2] In a radio interview, actor Martin Sheen commented, "Up until last year, I was very dubious...I did not want to believe that my government could possibly be involved in such a thing, I could not live in a country that I thought could do that—that would be the ultimate betrayal. However, there have been so many revelations that now I have my doubts."[3] How and why could citizens of a democratic state believe that their own government would murder or allow others to destroy them?

This book argues that the roots of these kinds of beliefs lie much deeper than 2001. Americans' mistrust of government goes back to the nation's founding. The United States is, after all, a country founded in a revolution against government excess. Conspiracy thinking itself also has deep roots within the U.S. body politic. New, however, is the extent to which American public discourse is now permeated by the language of conspiracy.

Conspiracy theories, present on the fringe of American politics since the nation's founding, became an accepted part of popular discourse in the late 20th century. While once these views might have been considered the harmless and eccentric beliefs of a few, now they are neither. Paradoxically, they foster both political apathy and its opposite, political extremism, and significant numbers of people believe they provide reasonable explanations for economic, social, and political events. Talk of conspiracy is everywhere, from Tea Party assertions about Obama's birthplace[4] to accusations regarding George W. Bush's political agenda and concern that the Federal Emergency Management Agency has established secret concentration camps to imprison American citizens.[5] The history of this way of thinking about politics has much to tell us about our current political environment and its cleavages. This book is therefore not an effort to assess the truth of any of these conspiracies. Instead, it reflects upon the history of conspiracy theory as the history of a particular way of thinking about the world. It also examines why conspiracy theory has become more prominent within the United States in recent years.

Conspiracy Thinking

The word "conspire" literally means "to breathe together," and its connotation—men and women invisibly but intimately connected—fits the word's usage across the centuries. Historically, the term referred to individuals coming together to engage in a "criminal, illegal, or reprehensible" plot.[6] Its usage, however, changed slightly but definitively in the 20th century. Rather than focusing on a small band of conspirators, the term instead came to refer most commonly to the belief that some covert agency "political in motivation and oppressive in intent" was directing world affairs.[7] Today, the word "conspiracy" most likely conjures up in our imagination the image of a small cabal of individuals that somehow controls the political and economic world, and might also manipulate every aspect of our lives. While these two types of conspiracy thinking are related, one of the arguments of this book is that the distinction between them is meaningful, and that the growing importance of superconspiracies is particularly significant.

Today, conspiracy theories concerning single events still exist, and single events are often the subject of a multiplicity of such theories. Marilyn Monroe's suicide, for example, fostered the development of many theories that contradict the official autopsy results, and subsequent investigations by the authorities. Many of them name Robert Kennedy as the central figure responsible for her death. Each of those theories identifies different figures (Marilyn's psychiatrist, the Secret Service, the FBI, and even the Communists) as carrying out his plans. Other theories suggest that J. Edgar Hoover ordered her murder. Still others claim she was killed by the Mafia working with the Kennedy family, aiming to hurt the Kennedys or aiming to help the Kennedys.[8] An entire body of literature exists, for example, that suggests that Marilyn was murdered because the Kennedy brothers had told her the real truth about UFOs and Roswell. One such theorist writes, "If Monroe was indeed aware of President Kenndy's [sic] secret visit to see downed alien life and technology, and was about to blow the whistle, then she was a security threat. She directly jeopardized the Kennedy brothers [sic] efforts to restore direct Presidential oversight of extraterrestrial related issues. The stakes couldn't be higher."[9]

In contrast, "superconspiracies" identify a single malevolent force at work behind a network of organizations attempting to consolidate control of all meaningful political and economic activity.[10] Typically, they identify the shadowy masterminds behind these plans as mysterious groups such as the Knights Templar, Freemasons, or the Illuminati. Every superconspiracy identifies its own combination of conspirators; a small sample of the most popular of these includes specific individuals in the American government, Saudi oil interests, Jews, lizards in the center of the earth, extraterrestrial spirits invading human bodies, Osama bin Laden's Masonic connections, and a business lobby of "Freemasons loyal to the Zionists."[11] Superconspiracies have a life in mainstream political discourse that is both curious and profoundly troubling. A belief that individuals conspired to cause a single event may indicate a lack of information or perhaps a moderate and healthy skepticism, but belief in a superconspiracy suggests that perhaps the individual concerned has lost his sense of personal and political efficacy.

These two forms of conspiracy belief are not, however, clearly distinct. Groh suggests that modes of historical explanation exist on a spectrum, with conspiracy at one end and science at the other.[12] It is possible, he argues, that the degree to which individuals resort to conspiracy to explain the world also exists on a spectrum. Some individuals might use it in a very limited way, while others might use it to explain quite simply everything, a view that implies that there are some conspiracy beliefs that are not as harmful as others. In 1997, for example, Diana, Princess of Wales, was killed in a terrible Paris car crash, along with her boyfriend, Dodi Al-Fayed; the official French inquiry found that the driver of their car had consumed a significant amount of alcohol and was driving above the speed limit, and that his passengers were not wearing seat belts. A number of individuals, including Mohamed Al-Fayed, Dodi's grieving father, claimed that "the British Establishment" wanted Diana and Dodi dead. He complained that the inquests were incomplete and inaccurate: "The jury have found that it wasn't just the paparazzi who caused the crash, but unidentified following vehicles. Who they are and what they were doing in Paris is still a mystery."[13] Conspiracy theorists have pounced upon Al-Fayed's observations. A limited conspiratorial interpretation of these events might be that Diana had "finally had enough of the Windsors" and was assassinated before she could reveal their darkest secrets.[14] A more extreme and problematic conspiratorial view is that "the death of Diana was engineered by the satanic thirteen interrelated family bloodlines collectively known as the Illuminati and that the thirteenth pillar [of the tunnel] was deliberately selected as the point of impact."[15] This is a significantly expanded conspiracy theory that involves the British and French Secret Services, by implication the British and French governments, as well as the Illuminati and the Freemasons, secret organizations that in this view are capable of orchestrating the broad sweep of world history, down to its finest details. Here, the first type of conspiracy thinking suggests a kind of extreme suspicion of the British monarchy, and in the case of Mohamed Al-Fayed, a father's grief. The second type evidences faith in unseen forces of history that can somehow control the details of everyday existence, down to which pillar a speeding car hits in a Paris tunnel. It implies a particularly pathological way of understanding history and politics.

Barkun contends that while more limited conspiracy beliefs may seem harmless, there is no safe conspiracy theory because contemporary conspiracy theories evidence a "dynamic of expansion." Accepting one such theory inclines one to accept another. This process means that one moves from the explanation of one event to eventually arrive at a "superconspiracy," the view that a single, all-powerful, evil force is directing numerous conspiracies that are hierarchically linked together and directed.[16]

These arguments are supported by surveys of conspiracy believers. In 1994, Ted Goertzel found that people who believe in one conspiracy theory are likely to believe in others, and that those theories do not have to be thematically or logically related.[17] Goertzel's survey questioned respondents regarding theories as diverse as: "the American government deliberately put drugs into the inner city communities"; "the Japanese are deliberately conspiring to destroy the American economy"; and "Ronald Reagan and George Bush conspired with the Iranians so that the American hostages would not be released until after the 1980 elections."[18] His findings are supported by two more recent studies. A 1999 study of university students found that those who had adopted specific conspiratorial theories did not just believe in one conspiracy; they believed in an average of 5.7 conspiracies.[19] These conspiracies were unrelated, and extremely diverse, including arguments that the United Nations is taking over the United States, that the American government has engaged in cover-ups of alien landings, that water fluoridation is a conspiracy, and that a cabal of Jews has taken control of the banking system.[20] A more recent British study made a similar finding. Following September 11, 2001, researchers found that one of the principal traits of those who believed the events of that day were the work of conspirators was belief in other conspiracy theories.[21] That is, "believing that John F. Kennedy was not killed by a lone gunman, or that the Apollo moon landings were staged, increases the chances that an individual will believe in 9/11 conspiracy theories."[22] The authors of both studies point out that conspiracy theories provide easily accessible explanations for events that might threaten an individual's belief system.

For Barkun, these types of links are problematic. He argues that as conspiracy beliefs expand, so does believers' perception of the domain of evil. The number of conspiracy participants and their powers increase. An apparently benign belief can be one step toward the acceptance of a more malevolent conspiracy theory. Indeed, Barkun points out that many members of the UFO subculture have come to believe that the explanations for history and politics provided in the *Protocols of the Elders of Zion* are true.[23] At gatherings of the militia movement, for example, the *Protocols* are openly supported.[24]

The document known as the *Protocols of the Elders of Zion* is a prominent anti-Semitic conspiracy document, and for that reason, it is worth considering briefly here. Written by Russia's czarist secret police sometime before World War I, it is perhaps the world's most famous forgery. The *Protocols* allegedly documents a secret meeting of Jewish leaders who are planning to take over the world and institute totalitarian control over every aspect of human existence.[25] Despite the fact that the document is a complete fabrication, it was published across Europe and Asia as a true account. In the United States, Henry Ford sponsored its publication, and it sold hundreds of thousands of copies.[26] As Barkun suggests, a most notable feature of the *Protocols* is its adaptability and malleability; from its first appearance onward, it has morphed into a variety of forms (linking various combinations of secret societies to the Jews' supposed nefarious schemes). In 2002, for example, Egyptian television aired a 41-part television series that dramatized the forged document. Every episode began with the same introduction:

> Two thousand years ago the Jewish Rabbis established an international government aiming at maintaining the world under its control and suppressing it under the Talmudic commands, and totally isolating them from all of the people. Then the Jews started to incite wars and conflicts, while those countries disclaimed them. They falsely pretended to be persecuted, awaiting their saviour, the Messiah, who will terminate the revenge against the Goyim that their God, Jehovah, started.[27]

In the architecture of superconspiracy theories, the *Protocols* provides a readily accessible link to anti-Semitism.

Believers in superconspiracies are also likely to be more rigid in their beliefs than those who adopt only single-event conspiracy theories. The scope of a superconspiracy means that the final conflict believers envision can only be concluded with an "Armageddon-like" battle.[28] In addition, they are less likely to give up their beliefs. Their belief system is not just one of many that compete in the marketplace of ideas, but the expression of absolute truth.[29] The internal construction of all conspiracy theories is hyper-rational and effectively impossible to disprove. This is particularly true of superconspiracies that purport to explain everything. All actors and events are active in the conspiracy; events that appear not to fit its pattern actually do, but in hidden ways.

As Barkun points out, accepting a conspiracy is ultimately not a judgment based on proof, it is a leap of faith.[30] When they are considered in this way, conspiracy theories resemble religious doctrines. They identify a hidden power that is moving history toward its conclusion, and ultimately they rely on believers' faith—their conviction—rather than scientific evidence. In the words of Matthew Gray, conspiracism is therefore "the act of developing and sustaining a discourse, usually a counter-discourse, that challenges conventional or accepted explanations for events, and that uses weak, flawed, or fallacious logic, seeks to convince through rhetoric and repetition rather than analytical rigor and most often aims to develop a theory that is broad, even universal in scope."[31]

Barkun argues that all conspiracy theories share three characteristics. They assert: (1) that the world is governed by design and purpose, and therefore there is no accident or coincidence; (2) that "nothing is as it seems," and therefore appearances cannot be trusted; and (3) that "everything is connected," and therefore even those entities that may on the surface appear to be diametrically opposed in ideology or political goals are working in concert.[32] In other words, the architecture of conspiracy belief systems reassures believers that their lives are meaningful and that they exist in a meaningful universe. All conspiracy theories suggest that real power is exercised in hidden ways, and that even those who appear to wield significant political and economic influence—the president of the United States, or the Al-Fayed family, for example—may be its victims. Likewise, conspiracy theories identify unusual and hidden alliances among political actors. Prior to the end of the Cold War, for instance, the American Liberty Lobby suggested that Communists and international bankers were in league to transform the world's governments to Communist dictatorships; adherents argued that Communism, while purporting to elevate the masses, in fact served the interest of international financiers.[33] Adapting their message for the times, the group's publications now argue that the bankers are in league with the American government to cover up the extent of Alaska's oil reserves: "The United States has more oil reserves than Saudi Arabia but this happy though shocking information has been covered up for years. The wells have been drilled, it's merely a matter of turning on the faucets to supply America's needs for 200 years."[34]

Another example of the startling connections sometimes made within conspiracy theories can be found in Dr. Boyd Graves's contention that at the height of the Cold War, American and Soviet scientists cooperated to create the Human Immunodeficiency Virus (HIV) to use against "undesirable" populations.[35] Related to this, Graves also argues that the American government discovered the cure for AIDS in 1997 (patent number 5676977) but has not allowed it to be manufactured and released because as yet, an insufficient number of people have died.[36]

For believers, counterintuitive alliances such as exist in Graves's theories provide evidence of the hidden nature of power. The conspirators are clever and able to pursue world domination in innovative ways, utilizing for example a ruse as complex as the Cold War to mask their plans. For nonbelievers, however, these alliances may seem extremely unlikely. Would Western business elites really cooperate with Communists in order to create dictatorships? Would the American government conceal oil wealth from its own population? Would the Soviet Union and the United States cooperate to create a deadly virus and delay releasing its cure? For conspiracists, the answer to these questions is always yes. In the view of the late Mae Brussell, for example, John Lennon's assassination was a complex conspiracy:

> His death was a well-constructed plot that involved careful manipulation of Mark David Chapman through hypnosis and mind control, starting with anti-Beatles propaganda when he became a Fundamentalist Christian. The church sucked him in, then the CIA took over. During Chapman's travels to London, Hawaii, Israel, Hong Kong and Korea, he was in the specific cities where the people identified with the Kennedy assassination all have bases. Why Lennon? The Reagan administration intends to make war on various soils, and John Lennon's energy was the greatest force for peace demonstrations. It was their desire to prevent a repeat of the demonstrations of the '60s.[37]

Within conspiracy belief systems, power operates in these unusual ways. In so doing, believers argue, it can successfully operate and continue undetected. In their view, if you do not see these connections, it is because you are part of the conspiracy, or because you have been duped.

A multitude of ancient and modern conspiracy theories therefore exists, purporting to explain everything from the death of Elvis to the American invasion of Iraq. This host of theories provides a veritable smorgasbord of explanations for politics and history, and within it, villains, victims, events, and the power that links them can be combined in a wide variety of ways. Believers can select the items they prefer, and link them together in whatever way they choose. The rich panoply of conspiracy theories suggests that it is perhaps the very idea of conspiracy and the structure of the belief system itself that draw so many people to this way of thinking.

A worldview wherein the personification of evil exists, working covertly, and exercising its power in a systematic way might be frightening to most of us. To others, however, it is reassuring. The world can be a terrifying place.

The evening news is rife with real horrors: terrorist acts, wars, and natural disasters. Random cruelty and injustice may be less threatening if they are understood to be the product of a known, identifiable enemy. Conspiracy theories provide believers with knowledge (and therefore a degree of control), an enemy against which to fight, and a purpose that is linked to a grand historical narrative.[38] As Jeffrey Bale comments, conspiracy theories explain why "bad things are happening to good people," and in so doing, they reaffirm a believer's potential to exert control over the future.[39]

While this aspect of conspiracy belief is part of its appeal, it also suggests a most important flaw in this way of thinking. While it is certainly true that elites and individuals can have an impact on politics and history, it is far from clear that they can know and direct the very course of world events. The historian Dieter Groh writes, "Men make their history themselves, but that which results as history is not *their* history in the sense that it is what they intended."[40] Because human beings exist in situations that are neither standardized, nor under our control, we cannot develop rules of action from them that would allow us to—literally—make the future.[41] Every human action can have both intended and unintended consequences. From the perspective of politics, the assumption that history can be controlled is also problematic. Hannah Arendt writes that the fundamental quality of human political life is natality, "the birth of new men and the new beginning, the action they are capable of by virtue of being born."[42] With every moment, new possibilities for the world emerge. They are unpredictable, and their implications are unknown: "The fact that man is capable of action means that the unexpected can be expected from him, that he is able to perform what is infinitely improbable."[43] For most historians and political theorists, therefore, conspiracy theories are fundamentally unsound. They presuppose that there exists a reason that is active in history, and that its purpose is knowable.

A second general error in the logic of conspiracy theories is their equation of coincidence with a meaningful plan. It is, for example, apparently possible to fold a $20 bill in such a way as to create a picture of the World Trade Center and Pentagon attacks of September 11, 2001, and apparently to fold other bills to show the sequence of events that day. Is this evidence that the government planned the attacks? Some people think so.[44] It is difficult to explain, however, why the government might telegraph a covert plan to commit mass murder and subsequently invade Afghanistan and Iraq on dollar bills. It does not seem like a reasonable action for a government that wished to keep its plans secret from the American people (to say nothing of why any individual might think that currency origami might be the best way to learn about government policy). While true believers might claim "there are no coincidences,"[45] a lack of evidence supporting these arguments makes it difficult for outsiders to believe this is the result of anything but chance.

Similarly, as Gray points out, political acts may be similarly interpreted.[46] In the context of the 2003 Iraq War, for example, then President George Bush's changing explanations for the invasion appeared curious. Was he covering the tracks of a major conspiratorial plot, or adjusting his story for the sake of political expediency? In the summer of 2010, President Obama found himself the center of controversy when he commented on a proposal to build an Islamic center and mosque near the site of Ground Zero. He later emphasized that he was not expressing support for the proposal but was instead only remarking on the fact that the United States Constitution provided for freedom of religious expression.[47] Were his comments evidence that he is in fact a Muslim, conspiratorially hiding his religious faith? A poll in August 2010 suggested that despite his history of church attendance, an increasing number of Americans were confused about his religious faith, and close to one in five Americans believe he is a Muslim.[48] Obama must balance dozens of interests on this question, and as a politician, perhaps a critical point is the importance of midterm elections and his own eventual electoral success. In addition, however, he must also consider the impact of his comments on the families of 9/11 victims, U.S. foreign policy, American Muslims, the Muslim Brotherhood, debates within Islam concerning the political meaning of that faith, and the nature of American international influence in the 21st century, to name only a few of the groups and debates upon which his remarks will have a meaningful impact.[49] Politicians frequently adjust their rhetoric and change their explanations as new information and/or public opinion develops. Such situations are the product of a lack of planning or the inability of individuals to control a situation, rather than evidence of a complete control over human history.

David Aaronovitch argues that this tendency of conspiracy theories to assume deliberate agency where chance or accident is more likely the cause should be understood as an inherent aspect of conspiracy thinking. He points out that it is simply more reasonable to believe that in 1969 men actually landed on the moon than to believe that thousands of people engaged in an elaborate plan to construct, maintain, and sustain a conspiratorial deception.[50] In this context, he comments that Occam's razor reminds us of another way of considering this problem. Aaronovitch translates the famous aphorism *Pluralitas non est ponenda sine neccisitate,* as "Other things being equal, one hypothesis is more plausible if it involves fewer numbers of new assumptions."[51] In other words, the simplest explanation is likely the most accurate explanation.

Conspiracy Theories: Paranoid Delusion or Politically Meaningful?

It is reasonable to question why anyone would come to understand history as the product of conspiracy. An easy answer might be that those who propagate and adopt conspiracy theories are paranoid. Their beliefs are rooted in a psychological problem that marks the way in which they interpret the world. Swami et al. found in their survey of British citizens that there were several character traits that correlated positively with belief in conspiracy theories. Those related personality factors include: a cynical attitude toward politics, defiance toward politicians, support for democratic principles, and an appreciation for new and unusual ideas. The study also found conspiracy belief to be negatively correlated with agreeableness, a factor the study's authors comment "likely stemmed from the association between disagreeableness and suspicion and antagonism towards others."[52] Goertzel's 1994 study produced similar findings, concluding that belief in conspiracies correlates with feelings of political alienation from the political system.[53] In addition, conspiracy theories helpfully provide a host of enemies toward which believers can direct their anger, and in this way function to resolve the tension that might exist between an individual's view of the world, and reality.[54]

The title of Richard Hofstadter's classic article "The Paranoid Style in American Politics" suggests that he argues that those who believe in conspiracy theories are simply irrational and suspicious. Hofstadter makes clear, however, that he is borrowing the clinical term "paranoid" for other purposes. While he argues that those who adopt conspiracy theories suffer from a deep sense of persecution, which they systematize in "grandiose theories of conspiracy,"[55] he distinguishes between the "clinical paranoiac" and the "paranoid political spokesman." Although they share some characteristics—both are "overheated, oversuspicious, overaggressive, grandiose, and apocalyptic in expression"—there are clear differences between them. Most notably, Hofstadter argues, the clinical paranoiac believes threats are being directed against him, but the political paranoiac believes the threats are directed against a nation, culture, and/or way of life.[56] For these reasons, political paranoiacs understand their convictions to be both unselfish and patriotic, and support them with a sense of "righteousness and moral indignation."[57]

Conspiracy thinkers often fall into this second category, and it is therefore more accurate and useful to consider how and why adopting conspiracy beliefs might appeal to the political sensibilities of particular individuals. First, as noted above, part of conspiracy theory's appeal—and one of its flaws—is the assumption that it is possible for human beings to make history, that is, to shape the world to their will. This way of understanding can be reassuring, for it begins with the assumption that it is possible for individuals to exercise some form of control over the world. This is also linked to the notion of identity. As James points out, where previously identity was ascribed, in modernity, we can create our own identity.[58]

Second, through their explanation of history, conspiracy theories provide their adherents with an explanation of how and why evil is at work in the world. Rather than addressing the complexity of human existence, however, they identify good and evil in clear-cut terms, and in so doing, also divide human beings into those who are good and those who are evil. In this world, shades of gray do not exist. Flanagan notes that this dualistic way of approaching politics is useful in times of war and for populist movements aiming to take power.[59] It clearly distinguishes between political allies and political enemies.

A third reason for the appeal of conspiracy theories lies in the security they provide to their adherents. As citizens of the modern world, we are accustomed to encountering change and crisis in our day-to-day lives. To varying degrees, we become adept at living with uncertainty. We learn to adapt to small scale personal change such as moving house or changing employment. We apprehend that at the national and international levels, change is also a constant feature of the political landscape. The events of September 11, 2001, shocked and saddened us, but it was the scope of their violence, and their implications that may have surprised us, not the fact that the nature of international politics could change. It is the case, however, that a small but significant minority of individuals do not, and perhaps cannot, adequately adapt. They are threatened by significant alterations to their lives.

In his study of conspiracy belief, Goertzel found that one factor that significantly correlated with conspiracy beliefs was concern about one's employment security.[60] One way in which individuals respond to these kinds of threats is to turn to belief systems that offer them comfort and security by providing an explanation for their problems and the promise that a solution exists that will allow things to be better in the future. While these types of ideologies are not always dangerous, they frequently have pathological aspects. An individual who loses his or her job and falls into this trap might be inclined to blame "immigrants swamping the job market," and conclude that the deportation of immigrants is an appropriate solution. Very few problems in the modern world, however, have such clear explanations, and it is rare that they have a clear-cut solution. Blaming a particular group or groups for one's own problems is a much easier intellectual enterprise than considering the ways in which forces of the global economy have transformed the employment market.

An important point of clarification here is that although conspiracy theories may at first seem to provide a very simple explanation for political events, when one considers them carefully, it becomes apparent that they often paint a picture of the world that is extremely complex. A number of conspiracy theories exist, for example, that suggest some type of international Jewish conspiracy was behind the events of September 11, 2001.[61] One such theory claims that 4,000 Jews were warned to stay home from work on that day on the instruction of the Israeli Secret Service, a theory apparently based on a *Jerusalem Post* article that stated 4,000 Israelis were believed to have been near the World Trade Center and the Pentagon on the day of the attacks.[62] Although this explanation appears simple, if it were true, it would rely on the collusion of over 4,000 individuals to keep the truth secret, and a vastly complex chain of power relationships. The official story is much simpler.[63] Once again, Occam's razor suggests the conspiracy theory is unlikely.

Groh suggests that at the level of everyday perception, it is only an individual's "healthy common sense" that prevents him or her from adopting conspiracy theory as a mode of explanation for events.[64] In that sense, conspiratorialists are not abnormal. Every human being might at any time be tempted to cross the line and utilize conspiracy as explanation. It is, he writes, a "permanent temptation,"[65] and we are all potentially susceptible to such belief systems. Indeed, the leap to conspiracy theory may not be as great as we imagine. Conspiracy theories are internally consistent, and like more scientific understandings of the world, they begin with the assumption of explicit causality. Indeed, they surpass reality in terms of their logical consistency. Individuals and events are connected in ways that are more coherent than in the real world, where errors and ambiguity exist.[66] Nesta Webster, arguably the most influential conspiracy theorist of the 20th century, became convinced that the world was governed by conspirators while she researched the French Revolution. She argued that since it was impossible for the masses to create such an upheaval themselves, it was therefore reasonable to ask "by whom was it made?"[67] She concluded that a Jewish conspiracy controlling such forces as "Grand Orient Masonry, Theosophy, Pan-Germanism, International Finance, and Social Revolution" was involved, and this conspiracy was the cause of all threats to Britain and "Christian civilization." Webster developed an elaborate schematic table that purported to illustrate secret links among groups as diverse as the Fenians and the British Conservative Party.[68]

Finally, as Hofstadter remarks, it is certainly true that history has been marked by a good number of conspiratorial acts. This is because all political behavior requires strategy; strategy may depend on secrecy; and anything that is secret might be described as conspiratorial.[69] In addition, real political conspiracies have existed. The "massive campaign of political spying and sabotage"[70] that constituted the Watergate scandal, for example, revealed the duplicity of the political leaders concerned and their capacity to engage in illegal conspiratorial behavior to accomplish their political goals. As Johnson points out, however, real conspiracies are not the rigid systems of power that conspiracy theorists believe exist. They are comprised of people, not "mindless pawns of evil."[71] The Watergate conspiracy is notable, but so too is its discovery and aftermath. Individuals—even those involved in illegal conspiracies—often behave in unpredictable ways, and in democracies, this capacity can be fully expressed. Participants or observers to a conspiracy may decide to speak up and reveal what has happened, as Deep Throat did in the case of Watergate. In a similar vein, Aaronovitch argues that the most effective conspiracy involving the American government was the 1985–86 Iran-Contra Affair.[72] This conspiracy saw senior members of the Reagan administration circumvent a congressional prohibition on support for the Nicaraguan Contras by selling weapons to Iran. It was intended both to secure the release of American hostages in Iran and provide support for the Contra rebels in Nicaragua. The elaborate scheme unraveled, and eventually 14 people were charged in the affair. Again, reality proved too difficult to control.

Popular culture has also absorbed these ideas. From the early 1990s onward, the idea of conspiracy has featured in a variety of media. Chris Carter's *X-Files* franchise brought conspiracy theory to American prime-time television for almost 10 years, quickly becoming part of the cultural landscape. As Joyce Millman wrote for the *New York Times,* "It hauntingly captured the cultural moment when paranoid distrust of government spilled over from the political fringes to the mainstream, aided by the conspiracy-theory-disseminating capability of the Internet. With its high-level cover-ups, Deep Throats and adherence to the watchwords "Trust no one," *The X-Files* tapped into still-fresh memories of Iran-Contra and Watergate, not to mention Ruby Ridge and Waco."[73] Building on a surging mistrust of government, the program followed two FBI agents, Fox Mulder and Dana Scully, as they investigated cases that involved extraterrestrial intervention in world affairs, and which seemed to suggest that a secret group of government officials and business executives were working together toward nefarious ends. Interestingly, *The X-Files* is one of the first appearances in popular culture of the superconspiracy form; the program's story lines involve evidence going back in history thousands of years.[74]

More recently, Dan Brown's novel *The Da Vinci Code* and its follow-up, *The Lost Symbol,* have further extended the reach of conspiratorial thinking. Brown's stories concern the adventures of Harvard symbologist Robert Langdon, whose esoteric knowledge draws him into the inner workings of the Illuminati, Freemasons, and Knights Templar, and there is no denying the books' appeal. *The DaVinci Code* sold over 80 million copies worldwide, and on its first day of release, *The Lost Symbol* was the fastest selling adult book ever, with sales of over one million in the United States, the United Kingdom, and Canada.[75] The books purport to reveal the hidden truths of the Knights Templar, the Freemasons, the Illuminati, and that other secret society with a worldwide reach, the Roman Catholic Church. Dan Brown was aware he was writing fiction, but the publicity his work received, and the response of these institutions to the charges made against them by characters in the books, suggested that at least in some people's minds, the books were either too close to the truth or a threat for other reasons. In Britain, the Catholic "DaVinci Code Response Team" commissioned a survey concerned with gauging the effect of the book. It found that of those who had read the novel, 60 percent believed that its claim that Jesus fathered a child with Mary Magdalene was true.[76] The response by the Catholic Church in the United States was similar. The United States Conference of Catholic Bishops launched the website Jesusdecoded.com to counter the book's claims. Those with the conspiracy mind-set, however, were unlikely to be convinced—in fact, they were more likely to have their beliefs reaffirmed—by such a campaign. *The Da Vinci Code* movie struck a similar chord.

Dozens of other conspiracy-oriented movies have been made, in the post–Cold War, post-Watergate era, and many of them have been marked by, if not antigovernment themes, then certainly the message that one ought to be suspicious of politicians and one's government. Barry Levinson's *Wag the Dog;* Michael Mann's *The Insider;* Steven Spielberg's *Minority Report;* Oliver Stone's *JFK* and *Nixon;* Andy and Larry Wachowski's *The Matrix;* and of course, Richard Donner's *Conspiracy Theory* all fall into this category. With the decline of the Soviet Union as a dependable foil for United States' interests, one suspects, a conspiracy-minded public's adoption of the government as the people's enemy became a particularly appealing plot line.

Conspiracism's infiltration of popular culture has increased familiarity with the content of specific conspiracy theories and arguably also increased their acceptance as a mode of political explanation.[77] In addition, the Internet has spread conspiracy theories further and faster than ever before. Barkun argues that this method of transmission also makes them a more respectable form of explanation. Conspiracy theories were once a form of stigmatized knowledge; the larger political community marginalized them. Through the Internet, however, they have moved closer to the mainstream. With millions of pages of information and no means for its readers to distinguish between fact and fiction, the Internet blurs the line between these two realms. As a result, once stigmatized forms of knowledge may become indistinguishable from more mainstream ways of thinking.

Barkun notes that through popular culture, individuals who are inclined to think in terms of conspiracies are given further reason to do so, and through the Internet, they are provided with a smorgasbord of options as well as a means of disseminating their own views.[78] Jodi Dean, in fact, goes so far as to suggest that conspiracy theories are a reasonable form of political expression. She argues that a shared conception of "reality" does not exist, so that conspiracy theories are perhaps plausible ways to understand the world and must be taken seriously. Thus, conspiracy is no longer part of the "lunatic fringe, but a "vehicle for political contestation."[79] While Dean's arguments are interesting, this book takes the position that although conspiracy theories very often spring from legitimate political grievances and/ or are the result of significant political concerns, their content and structure are problematic and rarely reflect the genuine condition of political existence.

Another reason for the prevalence of conspiracy theories is that modern governments are extremely complex entities and require significant bureaucracies in order to function. The complexity of these systems can make their behavior occasionally incomprehensible to their citizens. Government policies may be influenced by specific interests and marked by contradictions. In addition, civil servants may not always effectively or consistently implement those policies. This situation lends itself to conspiratorial explanations. If one cannot understand how governmental decisions are made and policies implemented, one might assume that an elite conspiracy of individuals is indeed directing a government's behavior, and as Hofstadter points out, in democracies, this is particularly problematic.[80] This possibility, coupled with high-profile political events in which government appeared ineffective (for example, Hurricane Katrina, the events of September 11, 2001, and even the Deepwater Horizon oil spill in the Gulf of Mexico), contributed to making conspiracy theories appear to be reasonable explanations for the government's lack of response to the chaos of human existence.

Conspiracy theories have long been a part of American political life, but there are particular historical periods in American history when they have developed into a more significant part of public discourse. The remainder of this book attempts to answer the question of why this is the case, and it explores the significance of this phenomenon. An important part of this endeavor is a consideration of the content of those beliefs. The 20th century was littered by the emergence of a multitude of single-event conspiracy theories, but the real innovation in conspiracy thinking was the rise of superconspiracies. While conspiracy thinkers had previously identified the Knights Templar, Freemasons, and Illuminati as conspirators, it is really only in the past 100 years that these three groups have found their way into the majority of modern superconspiracies. The historical record of the Templars, Freemasons, and Illuminati is enlightening, for it illustrates that these groups and their leaders are very different from the place they hold in 20th-century conspiracy theories. The distance between reality and their symbolic meaning reveals much about the appeal of modern conspiracy theories.

Chapter 2

The Big Three: The Knights Templar, the Freemasons, and the Bavarian Illuminati

Conspiracy thinking pervades our social world, to such an extent that we might think that it has always been a part of the way people talk about politics, economics, and society. Modernity and globalization challenge societies in particular ways that seem to encourage the development of conspiracy theories. As noted in the previous chapter, however, while political conspiracies have likely always existed, the superconspiracy theories popular today are relatively recent inventions. Their immediate origins lie in the early 20th century, and they were nourished by the changing social structure of the declining British Empire. Although superconspiracy theories are therefore a recent innovation, their historical roots are deep, and believers search history for evidence of their influence over the modern world.

Among the panoply of conspirators identified by modern theories, three groups in particular stand out: the Knights Templar, the Freemasons, and the Bavarian Illuminati. Amidst the government officials, aliens, lizards, and other peculiar entities that populate many modern conspiracy theories, these groups are particularly noticeable. First, we know with some certainty—even though they are/were secret societies—that they actually existed, and second, they have, if conspiracy thinkers are correct, been working through their evil plans for hundreds of years. Finally, they play a critical role in so many conspiracy theories that their presence is impossible to ignore. Why do these ancient organizations dominate so many modern conspiracy theories? The answers to this question help to explain the emergence of conspiracy theory and the continuing popularity of the conspiracy belief structure. This chapter therefore begins with a brief historical examination of each of the "Big Three": the Knights Templar, the Freemasons, and the Bavarian Illuminati. As J. M. Roberts writes, it is difficult to discern the history of secret societies because the line between their "mythological and positive history" is frequently unclear.[1] The many and spectacular deeds for which they are supposedly responsible are only related in a tangential way to the historical record, and sometimes the historical record itself is only "semi-real." While this account of their histories is unlikely to convince conspiracy believers—as noted in the previous chapter, their convictions are a matter of faith, not rational thought—such an examination is important, for it illustrates the interesting similarities in their origins and the function they served in their respective political communities. These commonalities suggest good reasons why, in times of political and economic change, these groups have come to dominate the popular imagination.

The Knights Templar

The first and most ancient of the Big Three is the Poor Knights of Christ and of the Temple of Solomon. Commonly known as the Knights Templar, this group came to widespread mainstream attention through Dan Brown's novel, *The Da Vinci Code*. In that fictional story, the Templars and their disappearance provide an elaborate screen for the Priory of Sion, a yet more secret organization, supposedly charged with protecting the secret bloodline of Jesus's and Mary Magdalene's offspring. McConnachie and Tudge describe the plot as "codswallop," and Aaronovitch makes a similar suggestion, but this mythological history was compelling to millions of people. The real history of the group is just as interesting but somewhat less dramatic.

The Knights Templar began in the early 1100s when a French nobleman and nine of his companions dedicated themselves to the protection of Christians traveling to and from Jerusalem during the Crusades. The Templars were therefore first a religious community. They did, however, practice secret rites of initiation and prayer, activities that made them suspect, and eventually helped lead to their downfall. In many ways, the Templars are the symbolic prototype for all secret societies. They were both priests and soldiers, an innovative combination that Pipes contends was particularly threatening to individuals outside the Order. Their embodiment of both heavenly and earthly authority was a new and, for many, a troubling development. Ultimately, too, they accumulated significant wealth, a fact that further added to their aura of mystery and power. For a time, they were even bankers to French royalty.[2] Their tremendous wealth further increased outsiders' suspicions of the Order. Their proximity to political power, and their wealth and prestige transgressed feudal norms. In addition, it led outsiders to question their piety.

The Templars were therefore extremely successful, but eventually they met with a significant military defeat. In 1291, Acre, the last Crusade stronghold, fell, and Templar fortunes changed. In the early 1300s, as they prepared to launch another crusade, the French monarchy and the Church moved against them. The monarchy confiscated the Templars' wealth and imprisoned and tortured its members. Eventually, Philip IV found the Templars guilty of apostasy, and their leader, Jacques de Molay, was burned at the stake.[3]

The secretive Knights Templar had religious authority, economic resources, and political power. Not only did they challenge the social order of their day, but they also created a new kind of political actor, the priest knight. In so doing, the Templars came to represent a power beyond the control of traditional authorities, and these qualities ensured their place in history.

After their abrupt loss of authority, the Templars apparently disappeared from political life. In the minds of conspiracy theorists, however, they live on. Indeed, the Templars cast a deep shadow over modern conspiracy theories, and they can, in Umberto Eco's words, be found everywhere.[4] Different conspiracy theories understand the Templars' role in different ways, but the Knights play a pivotal role in the history of conspiracy thinking. A number of modern conspiracies, for example, identify the Knights Templar as pivotal players in the French Revolution. Frequently, these types of theories argue that it was the Templars' leader, Jacques De Molay, who directed the Freemasons to make the Revolution.[5]

Some theories also identify the Knights Templar as closely involved in more recent events, for example, September 11, 2001. Barkun notes that in "The Twin Towers and the Great Masonic Experiment," Richard Hoagland argues that the numerological meaning of the date September 11, 2001, reveals a link to the number 11 (each tower had 110 floors; one was struck by Flight 11, etc.). This information is then linked to the year 1118, a number with integers that total 11, and evidently the year the Knights Templar were recognized by the Vatican. Hoagland then concludes that the events of September 11, 2001, were in fact an attack by the Islamic Order of Assassins against the Knights Templar and the Freemasons.[6]

Today, various instantiations of the Knights Templar do continue to exist, and the Order claims to have a membership that numbers three quarters of a million. Its branches are not, however, centers of military power, and while its members may be wealthy, they do not threaten the established economic system. A prospective member of the Order must profess a belief in "Christian ideals, a belief in the Holy and Undivided Trinity and [be a person] who seeks the society of men pledged to deeds of Charity, the practise of Christian virtues and the promotion of Christ's Kingdom on earth."[7] Membership in the modern Knights Templar does, however, require applicants to already be members of York Rite Freemasons and to have reached the level of "Master Mason." It is therefore appropriate to next engage in an examination of the Freemasons. Conspiracists would hold that the link between these organizations suggests some nefarious plan. A consideration of the Freemasons' historical evolution reveals that this is likely not so.

The Freemasons

The history of the Freemasons reveals that it is marked by similar themes to that of the Knights Templar. Roberts's assertion that secret societies' real history differs substantially from their mythological history is undoubtedly the case for the Freemasons, the organization perhaps most often identified at the center of both early and modern conspiracy theories. The Freemasons are apparently in cahoots with Rotary and Lions Clubs and involved in plots ranging from the distribution of aspartame to control the human mind ("*Aspartame* is such a blatantly High Masonic term. You have the *asp,* which is the serpent; of course, of Cleopatra, she did herself in with them; and you have tame. See, you *tame* the person—and you do that by going for the brain cells. However, who was the one who got it through into the US Food and Drug Administration? It was Donald Rumsfeld")[8] to the death of Pope John Paul I,[9] to an apparent plot to spread Zionism.[10] Understandably then, the legends surrounding the group's origins and history are many, and they have overwhelmed the popular imagination. It is the case, however, that the significantly more mundane reality of its development in a rapidly industrializing Britain is perhaps more interesting and suggests where the movement's real significance and power truly lie.

Some Masonic histories—and indeed, a number of conspiracy theories—claim that the movement's history reaches back to biblical times, specifically to the construction of Solomon's Temple, and includes an assortment of other groups and events such as the Eleusinian mysteries, the Essenes, the Druids, and Roman cults.[11] The predominantly mythological *Constitutions of the Free-Masons*, for example, asserts that:

> KING SOLOMON was GRAND MASTER of the LODGE at JERUSALEM and the LEARNED KING HIRAM was GRANDMASTER of the LODGE at TYRE and the INSPIRED HIRAM ABIF was MASTER OF WORK, and MASONRY was under the immediate Care and Direction of Heaven...after the Erection of SOLOMON's Temple, Masonry was improv'd in all the neighboring Nations; for the many artists employed about it, under HIRAM ABIF, after it was finished, dispers'd themselves into SYRIA, MESOPOTAMIA, ASSYRIA, CHALDEA, BABYLONIA, MEDIA, PERSIA, ARABIA, AFRICA, LESSER ASIA, GREECE, and other Parts of Europe, where they taught this liberal Art to the FREE BORN Sons of eminent Persons, by whose Dexterity the Kings, Princes, and Potentates, built many glorious Piles and became GRAND MASTERS, each in his own Territory...even in India.[12]

This document suggests that the principles of Freemasonry were blessed by God and that their spread around the world was undertaken as part of God's larger plan. These mythic stories were popular during the 18th century and helped to shape not only Masonic legends but also outsiders' views of the organization and its goals, particularly with respect to Freemasonry-related conspiracy theories.[13] Although this depiction of a group that has existed from almost the beginning of human history fits well with an organization purported to control the world, there is little evidence that Freemasonry and its lodges existed before the 17th century.

The first recorded mention of Freemasonry is of an Edinburgh military-oriented lodge in 1641, but the clearest indication of the movement's origins in Great Britain can be found in the Premier Grand Lodge of England, an entity created in 1717 by four London lodges. Its public emergence was followed by several other lodges across Great Britain openly declaring their existence.[14] In 1723, the organization published its first rulebook (*The Constitutions of the Free-Masons*, quoted above), and by 1748, there were over 150 lodges across England.[15] In 1776, Freemasons' Hall, on Queen Street,

London, opened; it included the Freemasons' Tavern, office space, and meeting rooms. In addition to Masonic activities, the Hall also hosted the meetings of many British philanthropic societies, including the British and Foreign Bible Society and the Anti-Slavery Society.[16]

Historical documentation of the Freemasons thus exists from the middle 17th century through to the present. The organization's continued presence in the social fabric of modern nations (there are Masonic lodges around the world, and in the United States, the group's membership, although in decline, still stands at over one million,[17] makes the questions of why and how the organization emerged important. Most relevant to our purposes here is that the answers to the questions help to explain why the Freemasons have played such an important role in modern conspiracy theories.

Social movements and organizations do not appear out of nowhere; they are the by-products of the societies from which they emerge. The social, economic, and political conditions that nourish them also foster their development in particular ways. They are therefore always marked by their generative conditions.[18] The Freemasons are no different. The political environment of a rapidly changing Great Britain, as well as the practical economic and social needs of the masonry profession, led to the development of an organization that was both a refuge from, and a vehicle of, that change.

While England had long been governed by a monarchy, the 17th and 18th centuries saw English politics fundamentally transformed. The combined impact of the English Civil War, the Glorious Revolution, and the Settlement Act of 1701 finally established the supremacy of Parliament, a development of critical importance in the establishment of Western democracy. It was followed by a century of civil conflict within the British Isles (including the Act of Union with Scotland and the subsequent Jacobite Rebellion) and explosive political events outside Britain that included the American War of Independence, Wolfe's defeat of Montcalm, the expulsion of the French from what is now Canada, and most notably for our purposes, the French Revolution.

Alongside this tremendous upheaval, economic and social changes occurred as well. The increased efficiency of British farm production meant that fewer workers were needed in agrarian pursuits; no longer required on farms, individuals moved to cities, a trend that increased the population's mobility and fostered further urbanization. The 1801 British census, for example, indicates that between 1775 and 1800, Manchester's population increased tenfold. Once a small parish, its population in 1801 had increased to 75,275 registered citizens by the close of the century.[19] From the patent of the steam engine in the middle 17th century onward, Britain was in the process of moving from a manual labor–based to a mechanized manufacturing economy. All of these changes played a role in the emergence of the Freemasonry.

As Roberts points out, among the craft-related organizations of the Middle Ages, Masons stand out. Most craftsmen belonged to town-based guilds, but the masons, due to the nature of their work, developed the lodge structure which "met the needs of a craft whose members were often itinerant, assembling sometimes for limited, even if for long, periods on building sites where no urban craft organization existed…[their] mobility led to the generalization of practices…and the evolution of rudimentary codes of mutual help and an internal discipline operating through the lodges."[20] While a guild hierarchy could maintain a close eye on its local members, and ensure standards and practices were upheld, masons had to develop a more flexible structure to undertake this role as they traveled to the far corners of Britain building cathedrals and halls. A significant problem was identifying whether or not other on-site colleagues were skilled tradesmen and members of their organization. The Masons developed secret signs and symbols for their members as a means of assessing outsiders and ensuring the standards of their profession. These secrets were not only a measure of an individual's standing as a mason (and thus maintaining a monopoly by limiting those who could practice the craft) but also a means of developing a spirit of brotherhood among a group of men who might often work far from their home and other masons.[21]

Initially, the masons' lodges were open only to practitioners of the craft. Members had to possess a sophisticated knowledge of Greek geometry and the skill to cut stone. In part because of their specialized knowledge and skill set, their trade was regarded as possessing a kind of special status. In addition, the masons' work was linked in practical terms to the centers of religious and political power. Priests and kings relied on masons and their knowledge to create the great and glorious stone buildings that symbolized their power.[22] In this way, the masons and their secret knowledge were linked to both divine and pragmatic political power. The most powerful of individuals—indeed the state and its institutions—depended upon them. Their knowledge and power could therefore be perceived as a threat to the social order. Symbolically, masons thus became revolutionary figures.

Their special knowledge, secret brotherhood, and proximity to power suggested they could transcend social boundaries and class.

The liminal status of the masons was further complicated by the shifting social and economic order of the early 1700s. The dynamic expansion of capitalist economies had begun to threaten the traditional guild structure (including Masonic lodges). Membership numbers began to decline, and in response, the Masonic brotherhood determined to admit new members: individuals who were not masons by trade but who wanted to have a part of the perceived Masonic cachet of secrecy and proximity to power. Typically, these individuals were members of the rising British middle class and brought to the organization both funds and increased political and economic influence. In turn, their presence transformed the movement from a trade organization to what was in effect a social club for men of the upper middle classes. In this way, traditional working "operative" Masonic lodges gradually declined. New "accepted masons" (individuals who were not working stonemasons) came to dominate the lodge structure, and eventually "speculative" masonry was born. Speculative Masonic lodges were those that were entirely nonoperative. As might be expected, with no real practical knowledge of stonemasonry's methods and practice, but attracted to the organization for its aura of specialized knowledge and its proximity to power, these new masons were free to create their own mythic language and symbols. They did so, building on the ancient language and work of the masons who were the forefathers of the organization. The rapid decline of operative masonry in the late 17th century was thus countered by an even more sudden and rapid expansion of speculative masonry. Indeed, by the time the London Grand Lodge was created, there was apparently only one operative lodge still in existence.[23] As noted above, the growth of these nonoperative, speculative lodges was phenomenal, with over 150 lodges in existence by mid-century. Such a sudden and widespread urge to join suggests that there was more at work here than an attraction to an atmosphere of mystery and power.

In this transformed movement, the traditional tools of masonry became central symbols, and these symbols embodied complex philosophical themes:

A stone, symbolizing man in the natural state, is to be shaped, polished, and fit into the building, which symbolizes the brotherhood of man. A first-degree Mason is responsible for 'preparing stones.' Upon initiation he is given a gavel, which symbolizes conscience; a chisel, which symbolizes education; and a twenty-four inch ruler, which symbolizes the hours of the day. After studying more Masonic lore, an initiate becomes a second-degree or Fellow Craft Mason and is given a square (mortality), a level (equality), and a plumb (rectitude)....Third-degree Masons are given a trowel to help cement the blocks together.... [i]t represents brotherly love.[24]

The mason's tools came to represent both major enlightenment themes and the idea of self-improvement.

These ideas help to explain the widespread appeal of the Masons. The lodges' transformation from operational to speculative masonry coincided with the transformation of British society. In the same brief span of time, Parliament became sovereign, and the Enlightenment's emphasis on education and science challenged the inward-looking, traditional, hierarchically based societies of Europe. In many ways, England was the crucible of those changes.[25]

The Masonic organization embodied the two major themes of this new age: first, the Enlightenment's emphasis on human rationality and its capacity to create a new and perfect world, and second, what was at the time a very revolutionary idea, the notion that an individual's station in life was not predetermined at birth. Through education, one could rise through society's ranks. Alongside the rapid expansion of capitalism, these forces were a potent mix. Billington argues that the most immediate appeal of Masonry was that it connected the notion of building construction and the possibility that a new society could also be made (or remade) in a more perfect way.[26] The Masons idealized the pragmatic rationality and the brotherhood of their predecessors, and their hope for the future embodied both these themes. When Freemasons can fully live the organizations' principles, "[t]he speculative Craft will then become operative, and the Ancient Wisdom so long concealed will rise from the ruins."[27]

The basic philosophical ideas manifest in Masonry's symbols underpinned a doctrine that emphasized equality, brotherhood, and self-improvement. To progress from "apprentice" to "journeyman," and then to "master," members had to acquire philosophic knowledge and demonstrate philanthropy, and any man who joined and learned the organization's symbols, rituals, and history could rise in its ranks. It was, as Billington writes, "a moral meritocracy."[28] The Masons' attention to status was related to the stratified nature of English society at the time. As Roberts points out, "It showed both the uneasiness of men increasingly aware of the artificiality of some social institutions which drove them to seek new social ties, and the status consciousness which was the reaction of those alarmed by signs of a new social mobility.[29]

Britain's new elite may have joined the organization to escape the country's rigid class structure, but in Masonry's doctrine, they recreated what they knew. Their organization, however, also reflected their appreciation for Enlightenment principles. They were not dangerous radicals but instead "middle class liberals who sought to improve society through free speech, elections, and secularism."[30] The Freemasons may have been revolutionary but only insofar as the ideals of democracy were revolutionary.

The Freemasons' lodges were in another way at the cutting edge of social organizations of their era. As discussed above, the England of the 1700s was marked by the polity's transition from monarchy to parliamentary democracy. It was also marked by significant religious conflict related to that transformation. While the Masonic lodges were a site where new democratic ideals could be discussed, they were also a place where they claimed religious conflict could be put aside. Freemasonry's Ancient Charges, for example, begin with a statement "concerning God and Religion":

> A Mason is oblig'd by his Tenure, to obey the moral Law; and if he rightly understands the Art, he will never be a stupid Atheist nor an irreligious Libertine. But though in ancient Times Masons were charg'd in every Country to be of the Religion of that Country or Nation, whatever it was, yet 'tis now thought more expedient only to oblige them to that Religion in which all Men agree, leaving their particular Opinions to themselves; that is, to be *good* Men *and true,* or Men of Honour and Honesty, by whatever Denominations or Persuasions they may be distinguish'd; whereby Masonry becomes the *Center* of *Union,* and the Means of conciliating true Friendship among Persons that must have remain'd at a perpetual Distance.[31]

In this way, the Masons claimed that the religious upheaval and conflict of the country as a whole was not to intervene in their lodges' affairs. This statement is not a declaration that members should abandon their religious faith (in fact, one cannot be a Mason and an atheist);[32] it is instead an assertion that good men of all faiths can come together as brothers. It might well be argued that the Masons' adoption of complicated symbols and rituals provided a new and unifying secular mythology for the organization's membership that replaced the divisive role of religion in society.[33] Indeed, Hall begins his *The Lost Keys of Freemasonry* with the assertion that "Freemasonry, though not a religion, is essentially religious. Most of its legends and allegories are of a sacred nature; much of it is woven into the structure of Christianity."[34] Instead of a Christianity that drove men apart, however, it was a form of religion that brought them together.

Despite this less than radical ideology, Masonry was condemned by the Roman Catholic Church. In 1738, the Vatican issued the first of 15 papal bulls condemning Freemasonry. The most recent statement on the compatibility of Roman Catholicism and membership in the Freemasons was in 1983, written by then Cardinal Joseph Ratzinger (now Pope Benedict XVI):

> [T]he Church's negative judgment in regard to Masonic association remains unchanged since their principles have always been considered irreconcilable with the doctrine of the Church and therefore membership in them remains forbidden. The faithful who enroll in Masonic associations are in a state of grave sin and may not receive Holy Communion.[35]

This prohibition was rooted in a number of factors related to Masonic doctrine, including a concern over Masonic support for rationalistic humanism and the assertion that Catholic Masons would have to exist in a "twofold mode," wherein they expressed their relationship with God in two forms, one that is merely humanitarian, and the other that is Christian.[36] By virtue of their Masonic beliefs, members of that organization must also in some way look upon their fellow Catholic communicants as outsiders. As a result, the Vatican has therefore consistently found Freemasonry to be irreconcilable with Catholicism.

Freemasonry and its doctrine of faith, brotherhood, and liberal democratic ideals spread quickly from England to the European continent and beyond. By the close of the 18th century, a rich tapestry of Freemason organizations existed across Europe, from Finland to Spain. Indeed, as Roberts points out, in urbanizing regions across Europe, the Masonic lodges provided a sense of community for their members, and a place of introduction for Masons who were visiting from other regions and/or countries. Casanova, for example, commented in his memoirs that Freemasonry allowed him to travel the world and, at the same time, enjoy the company of his social equals.[37]

Despite the variations among them, however, the Freemasons were united by their commitment to the ideas of the Enlightenment. The geographic reach of the movement saw the English Grand Lodge lose firm ideological control of the organization, and new variants of Freemasonry soon appeared among European countries, and within them. In France, for example, the late 1700s saw the Grand Loge de France, whose members were largely from the aristocratic class, in competition with French Grand Orient Freemasonry, which drew its membership from the professional and commercial class. In addition, what were called "lodges of adoption" appeared for women who desired to become members. In fact, Roberts suggests that on the eve of the French Revolution, there may have been as many as 100,000 French Freemasons; the organization effectively pervaded French culture and society.[38]

The most influential conspiracy theorist of the 20th century, Nesta Webster, argues that this was no accident, and that the Masons' nefarious plans were responsible for the French Revolution. Her accusations echo through modern conspiratorialists' belief systems, but the causal link she identifies is highly questionable—the Masons were too diverse and insufficiently organized to conduct a concerted campaign with a single purpose—but it is absolutely the case that the Masonic lodges *facilitated* the Revolution. This distinction is important, for it marks the line between reasonable political argument and conspiracy theory.

It is certainly the case that the Masons' emphasis on equality and brotherhood meant that its membership was likely a fruitful recruiting ground for the French revolutionaries. More significantly, however, as Billington points out, Masonry provided a critical metaphor for modern political revolutionaries, including those French men and women who hoped to overthrow their monarchical government and create a new republic: the idea that human beings, like architects and stonemasons, could build a new and better human society.[39] This belief structure was an innovation in the history of political thought and one of the modern era's most powerful inventions. Humans took upon themselves that which before it was believed that only God possessed: the power to make the world, and in so doing, make their own salvation. In this way, the French Revolution ushered in the era of political millenarianism. Human beings did not need to wait for God to intervene in history and end their suffering; instead, they could free themselves and create their perfect world.[40] The violently apocalyptic French Revolution embodied this urge, and the scope of the changes the revolutionaries enacted was far-reaching.[41] It was not just the replacement of a monarchy with a republic but also the disestablishment of the Roman Catholic Church, the replacement of traditional provinces with more geometric *départements,* the replacement of traditional laws with the civil code, and the replacement of traditional weights and measures by the more rationalistic metric system.[42] As Flanagan suggests, each of these changes may have been desirable in and of itself, but together, they represented an attempt to remake society from the ground up, in an effort to create a perfect future.[43] This secular millenarian effort was inherently totalitarian and unsurprisingly resulted in serious and sustained violence against dissenters.

In the religious sphere, this hope for a perfect future is often tempered by the fact that believers are content to wait for God to initiate the final age of history. Political millenarians, however, may be more dangerous, for they believe it is their destiny to transform the world. For this reason, they are often more violent than their religious compatriots,[44] and their attempts to remake the world are inherently totalitarian.

The French revolutionaries' desire for an entirely new world was perhaps best expressed in their creation of the Republican Calendar, which decreed that Year One began on September 22, 1792, the day of the Proclamation of the Republic, and that September 22 would be considered the first day of the year. The yearly calendar was now to be comprised of 12 months of 30 days; each month was divided into three 10-month units called decades; and every year included five extra days in order for the new Calendar to more accurately reflect the 365¼-day yearly cycle of the earth's movement around the sun. (Every fourth year was allotted a further extra day to make up the remaining time.)[45] This new Calendar, fantastically confusing as it is, aptly symbolized the revolutionaries' desire to begin a new era. It also evidenced the totalitarian implications of this way of thinking. Between 1793 and 1794, the regime executed thousands of men and women in a period that became known as the Reign of Terror. This campaign annihilated enemies, and through the use of fear, silenced critics and potential anti-regime conspirators. In this way, a political movement based on the ideals of liberty, equality, and humanity became a political regime that used terror and violence to subjugate its citizens.

At the time of the French Revolution, a variety of Masonic lodges existed in France. A number of revolutionary leaders were Masons, and Masonry provided a "symbolic vocabulary" for the Revolution.[46] These facts alone, however, do not allow us to conclude that Freemasonry planned the Revolution and coordinated its development. Instead, the events of the Revolution should perhaps incline us to conclude that even in the best conditions possible for directing a revolution—a political ideology whose time had come, and an oppressed and poverty-stricken population open to these ideas and willing to engage in violence to enact them—it is impossible to impose an idea on the world and have the world conform to your plans. Although many powerful individuals, including, no doubt, many Masons, intended that the French Revolution would create an eternal and glorious republic, those men could not make the entirety of the French political world conform to their will. The tremendous political upheaval that marked France in the years following the Revolution is evidence of this fundamental truth. During the next 100 years, the country certainly became a republic, but it was hardly stable; in that time frame, it also experienced constitutional monarchy, Napoleonic rule, and the Third Republic. In powerful and unexpected ways, the world resists attempts to shape it.

In a time of tremendous social upheaval in Europe, Freemasonry's lodges therefore provided a place where the emerging capitalist elite could discuss radical political ideas, including democracy, freedom, and equality, in a safe environment. The organization's emphasis on history and tradition, accompanied by the use of prominent ancient symbols, linked members to the past, while their focus on the ideas of the Enlightenment drew them into the future. The lodges served many practical purposes, including providing members with a sense of community in increasingly large urban centers. They also facilitated international mobility. As discussed above, Masonry's emphasis on brotherhood offered to its members who traveled an immediate and effective introduction to like-minded individuals in the countries that they visited.

In his classic analysis of social movements, Anthony Wallace argues that one can compare societies to living organisms. Like cells, they therefore work to maintain homeostasis, or a "steady state" at all times. During times of rapid social, political, and economic change and/or crisis, they develop mechanisms that help the community respond to new situations and challenges.[47] In Wallace's terms, these social groups are revitalization movements, "deliberate, organized, and conscious effort[s] to construct a more satisfying culture."[48] Such movements help to transform a society's way of understanding itself, and therefore facilitate its adaptation to changed circumstances.

The Freemasons and their lodges therefore played an important role in the development of 18th-century society, although perhaps not in the way conspiracy theorists would have us believe. As Dan Brown's character Robert Langdon points out in *The Lost Symbol,* the Masons were not a secret society so much as they were a "society with secrets":[49] they provided a confidential forum for the discussion of what were in the 18th century radical political ideas. For real political revolutionaries, however, the idea of a truly secret society was appealing. Indeed, it was not long before the Masons' innovations in organization were utilized by others.

The Order of the Illuminati

Freemasonry fulfilled the needs of individuals adjusting to a rapidly changing society. At the same time, however, it was an effective model of political organization, and it was only a matter of time before someone realized the potential of secret societies as strategic political actors. The person who did so was Adam Weishaupt, a law professor at the University of Ingolstadt, Bavaria. On May 1, 1776, Weishaupt, together with four of his friends, founded the Order of Illuminists. Freemasonry began in England as an outlet for a traditional society undergoing rapid change; Weishaupt's new organization played a similar role in Bavaria.

Eighteenth century Bavaria was still a traditional kingdom, and it was marked by the social, political, and religious hierarchies that were already changing elsewhere in Europe. Bavaria, however, had proved resistant to the powerful ideas of the French Enlightenment. Adam Weishaupt, a talented and motivated young scholar, set about to change that situation. Fueled by personal ambition and a desire for recognition, Weishaupt undertook to bring Enlightenment ideas to Bavaria. He created the Illuminati as a tool to help him accomplish that goal.

Educated at a Jesuit college, and employed at the Jesuit-dominated University of Ingolstadt, Weishaupt developed an appreciation for the religious order's political techniques and achievements. In his view, the Jesuits had maintained their power through effective domination of Bavaria's intellectual and cultural life. At the same time, however, he was frustrated by their influence over university teaching methods and curriculum, and in particular, their resistance to the ideas of the Enlightenment, and their hostility to non-Catholic instructional materials.[50] Weishaupt—who was well-connected within the university administration and confident of his continued employment despite his conflicts with the Jesuits—challenged them early on in his career. One of his earliest publications was a pamphlet that promoted the ideas of Protestant thinkers such as Hugo Grotius and Gottfried Leibniz, and his support for these scholars was an audacious move that angered his Jesuit colleagues.[51] Nevertheless, he was promoted to the position of Chair of Canon Law, a professorship that had been held by Jesuits for the previous century. Confident in his abilities, and popular with his students, Weishaupt began to criticize the university administration and his colleagues in lectures, and outside his employment, associated with ex-Jesuits and anticlerical radicals. As Roberts points out, these facts together suggest that he "was a familiar hazard of academic and collegiate life: the clever, cantankerous, self-absorbed, and self-deceiving bore" who in these activities also revealed his "taste for disciples and will to dominate."[52] Despite embodying the worst characteristics of the stereotypical academic, however, Weishaupt was redeemed by his vision of the future: he was enthralled with the ideas of the Enlightenment and believed they would liberate Bavaria from the chains of tradition.

Weishaupt's dream of a world dominated by human reason and science was prophetic. He understood that together these forces had the power to transform Western civilization. Indeed, over the next 200 years, they transformed the face of the world. Enlightenment ideas brought sweeping change to virtually every aspect of human existence. Science and technology altered the way we live, and the implications of these ideas also changed our political world. Reason, equality, and freedom became the foundation for new democratic regimes, including the United States of America. We now take these ideas for granted, but in Weishaupt's time, they were revolutionary. His colleagues recognized the threat they posed. For those who held power by virtue of religious institutions and tradition, equality and freedom were problematic. As a result, Weishaupt made enemies among his Jesuit colleagues at the university, and he stood to make real political enemies outside its ivory towers.

Weishaupt realized that his ability to disseminate Enlightenment ideas through the university was limited, and he began to consider how he might achieve a wider audience. Cognizant of how these ideas challenged Bavaria's governing class, he determined that the creation of a secret organization might be the most effective way to accomplish his goals. Politics requires strategy and sometimes therefore secrecy.

In such an environment, Weishaupt determined that a secret organization was the most effective way to spread Enlightenment ideas in Bavaria. He first considered Freemasonry as a possible means through which this could be accomplished but soon concluded that its elaborate doctrine, mythology, and symbols made it too conservative and apolitical. He wanted the most effective means possible to spread Enlightenment ideas in an oppressive political environment, and he concluded that for his purposes, an entirely new organization was necessary. He did not, however, begin with a blank slate. Weishaupt cleverly borrowed from the Freemasons, the world's most successful secret society, as well as from his bitter enemies, the Jesuits.

A vast body of conspiracy literature that asserts Weishaupt was a Jesuit and that his creation of the Illuminati was part of a complicated Jesuit plot to control the world.[53] There is, however, no evidence to support this charge. Indeed, even Nesta Webster, the doyenne of conspiracy theory, condemns this idea, commenting that Weishaupt "perpetually intrigued" against the Jesuits. Weishaupt admired the Jesuits; he was impressed that even dispersed around the globe they could follow a singular direction, and that as a group, they were not afraid to advance their own objectives at the expense of society's well-being.[54] As Webster writes, it was possible for Weishaupt to "imitate [Jesuit] methods whilst holding views diametrically opposed."[55] Weishaupt wished to end Jesuit influence—they were a barrier to the spread of freedom and equality—and he was willing to copy the order's tactics to do so.

Weishaupt also used Freemasonry effectively. He recruited from its membership, copied its structure, and utilized its complex symbolic codes for his own purposes. He joined a Masonic lodge in Munich in 1777 and from there began a campaign to recruit Illuminists from one of the German Masons' highest orders. Indeed, as Billington points out, Weishaupt appeared to use Masonry as a kind of training ground for Illuminism, and in the organization's later years, the two societies were fully integrated. One had to become a Mason before progressing through the Illuminati's ranks.[56]

In addition, the Illuminati made use of ancient symbols and ceremonies, again, like the Masons. Members took pseudonyms (Weishaupt became Spartacus), utilized Zoroastrian symbols to describe themselves and their ceremonies, and read classical political philosophy. As they moved through the movement's ranks, becoming "illuminated" through reason, they were gradually exposed to the Illuminati's true purpose: spreading the Enlightenment ideas of rationalism and egalitarianism. Only those within the movement's inner circle, the "Areopagus," were told of its political goals. The Illuminati were to infiltrate the social and political institutions of Bavaria, and from there create a Rousseauian world, wherein humanity would live in peace and brotherhood. In this perfected state, the divisions caused by society and organized religion would no longer exist.[57]

Like Freemasonry, the Order of the Illuminati was a response to the deterioration of traditional social structures and the emergence of modernity. Freemasonry, however, had emerged organically from traditional English social institutions. Weishaupt deliberately created the Order to achieve a specific political goal. Whereas the Masonic lodges had served as a place where individuals could discuss Enlightenment ideas, the Order of the Illuminati was effectively a political interest group that aimed to use those ideas to transform Bavarian society from a traditional hierarchical state, dominated by aristocrats and the Church, to a modern state governed by human reason and promoting equality and freedom.

It is difficult to determine the extent to which Weishaupt achieved his objective. The Illuminati certainly did not transform Bavaria into a perfected republican city-state. As historians point out, however, it is clear that many prominent Europeans joined the group. Intellectuals such as Goethe, Schiller, and Mozart, and statesmen such as Cobenzl, the Austrian foreign minister, and Hardenberg, the Prussian prime minister, were said to have been members,[58] and within Bavaria, it appears that both the political and educational establishments were peppered with Illuminati.[59] Despite its high-profile membership, however, ultimately the Illuminati were undone by the fact that the diversity of human experience and desire cannot be contained by a single political doctrine; the movement split over a disagreement regarding initiation ceremonies and political change in Bavaria.

Many conspiracy theorists contend that since the day that Weishaupt and his friends created the movement, the Illuminati has been the driving force behind modern history. Among their apparent accomplishments are a variety of major (and sometimes contradictory) political achievements. It is possible to find theories arguing that they oversaw international banking's creation of the *Communist Manifesto*, planned all the wars of the 20th century, engineered the events of September 11, 2001 (and in doing so fulfilled a long-term plan in accordance with biblical prophecy), and have controlled the behavior and policies of every U.S. president, including President Barack Obama.[60] As Wes Penre of the *Illuminati News* writes:

> More often than not the Illuminati sponsor both sides to have a game to entertain the ignorant public. They decide who will be the next president,

and they see to that their man wins, even if they have to cheat like they did in Florida when President George W Bush "won" over Al Gore. Even if their pre-elected candidate for some reason can't win and the other candidate does, they just go to Plan B, which is very well structured and prepared before hand, should this happen. So basically, no matter which candidate wins the race, THEY win.[61]

Other commentators suggest that if the Illuminati's powers seem super-human, perhaps it is because they are in league with the Grey Aliens.[62] The prominent role of the Illuminati in such a wide variety of conspiracy theories again suggests that it is perhaps the faith that someone or something is controlling history that appeals to believers. If this is so, the Illuminati's very lack of specific visible achievements might in fact be part of the reason for its popularity in conspiracy discourse.

In part, it is possible that the Illuminati's lack of visible impact is precisely the reason for its identification as an all-powerful villain engaging in intrigues that shape all aspects of human existence. It is effectively a blank canvas upon which conspiracy theorists can paint their own fears and suspicions. In addition to facilitating conspiracy belief by this lack of practical political accomplishment, Weishaupt and his small group of German intellectuals also engaged in creative organizational innovation. The nature of these changes also facilitates the wide—and wild—imputation of power and influence to the group. Weishaupt and his colleagues, for example, developed the concept of an organizational "double doctrine": the Illuminati's rank and file membership learned a belief system that was primarily theoretical and not particularly revolutionary, while those who moved through its hierarchy to its highest levels learned that it also had explicitly political goals.[63] This strategic move reflected the movement's overall purpose. The leadership hid the movement's real purpose from the majority of its members who gradually became "illumined" as they gained more knowledge. It was also a reasonably helpful political tactic. In an oppressive political environment, where ideas of freedom and equality threatened those who held power, the organization's real goals could be kept hidden.

For conspiracy theorists, the Illuminati's double doctrine is of particular importance. Their logic tells them that if these organizations can hide information from their own members, then clearly the organization's purpose is subversive and aims to undermine democracy. Following that assumption, the logic goes, such an organization must also be particularly adept at hiding its subversive goals from nonmembers. There are, however, problems with this logic. Across human history, leaders have devised political, military, economic, and business strategy and kept secrets from outsiders, both internal and external. In business, secrecy may protect a product or plan from competitors; in economics, a planned change to interest rates may protect a run on banks; in the military, it may protect soldiers' lives. In politics, secrecy may help leaders and elites more effectively achieve their goals. We might reasonably expect, therefore, that the leaders of modern democracies might plan specific strategies of which their political parties and citizens are not aware. For Weishaupt and the Illuminati, there were good reasons to keep the organization's political goals secret from the majority of members. The Illuminati planned a form of *democratic* revolution, and its strategy protected the membership from the state's wrath, and perhaps prolonged the organization's life.

Weishaupt's strategic abilities were also evidenced in the means he devised to mobilize a network of support. Pipes counts among the Illuminati's most important contributions Weishaupt's use of other societies' structures and membership. As noted above, Weishaupt modeled the Order on the structure of Freemasonry and went so far as to borrow its myths and symbols. In addition, he recruited members from the Freemasons and offered to give them special "advanced standing" to encourage them to leave the Masons for the Illuminati. If a man had attained a certain level in Freemasonry, he was admitted at an advanced level to the Illuminati hierarchy. Indeed, by the time of the Illuminati's demise, the two organizations and their membership did not just overlap, they were thoroughly interconnected. This arrangement served two purposes. First, it provided the Illuminati with a pool of possible new recruits already inclined to be hostile to clerics and fond of secret myths and symbols. Second, it was also a means to shunt off Illuminati members who "proved incapable" of acquiring full knowledge of the movement's goals.[64] Weishaupt clearly possessed a particular organizational genius.

The best laid plans, however, can go wrong, and the Illuminati soon began to suffer the consequences of both infighting and governmental attack. Weishaupt had come to rely on a German by the name of Baron Adolf Knigge, as one of his greatest recruiters. Indeed, he had quickly taken Knigge into his inner circle, and the man had an ever-increasing influence on the direction of the Illuminati's efforts. Knigge, however, differed with

Weishaupt on two key points: he was frustrated by the latter's insistence on a peaceful, philosophical revolution, and he was fond of mysticism, a tendency directly at odds with Weishaupt's doctrinaire rationalism. In addition, he was more sympathetic to the Church than was Weishaupt, a sentiment that may have sprung from his fondness for mysticism but was also related to his desire to recruit members from Germany.[65]

Weishaupt's and Knigge's differences eventually led to conflict, and it came to a head in 1784. The two men clashed over the development of new ceremonial practices for admission to the Illuminati's highest grade: Knigge developed elaborate, mystical ceremonies and Weishaupt felt those plans betrayed the purpose of the order. Ultimately, their disagreements led to Knigge's departure from the movement, threatening as he left that he would reveal the group's secrets. Unfortunately for Weishaupt, this internal dissension was just the beginning. Bavaria's reasonably liberal leader, Maximilian Joseph, was replaced by Carl Theodore, a man more conservative in outlook. He was threatened by the Illuminati's presence and banned all unauthorized societies. One year later, he proscribed the Freemasons and Illuminati specifically, citing concerns over their religious and political implications.[66]

Following this event, the Order of the Illuminati was disbanded. Weishaupt fled Bavaria, and apparently lived out the remainder of his years in Gotha. Before the dust could settle on this chain of events, a burgeoning Illuminati industry emerged. Weishaupt and Knigge each wrote their own account of the Illuminati and its activities (indeed, Weishaupt wrote three such books), and in the next five years, over 50 more publications on the Illuminati appeared. Some of these books purported to contain collections of documents confiscated by the government, and some aimed to present the organization's true history. Most, however, made outrageous claims with no evidence to support them. In one such volume, for example, Weishaupt was accused of both incest and infanticide, and in another, his organization was charged with poisoning the heir presumptive to the Duke of Zweibrucken, as well as encouraging masturbation, sodomy, and prostitution.[67] The notoriety of the main figures involved in the Illuminati, along with the political controversy and sexual allegations were then, just as today, good for book sales.

While Weishaupt may not have had immediate success, it is fair to say that in the long run, the Illuminati, like the Freemasons, spread the ideas of the Enlightenment indirectly. As Bernard Bailyn argues in his discussion of the liberal ideas that sparked the American Revolution, liberty is a contagion:

> The movement of thought was rapid, irreversible, and irresistible. It swept past boundaries few had set out to cross, into regions few had wished to enter.
>
> How infectious this spirit of pragmatic idealism was, how powerful—and dangerous—the intellectual dynamism within it, and how difficult it was to plot in advance the direction of its spread.[68]

Freedom is a powerful idea, and just as in America, once it had been unleashed in Bavaria, it could not be contained. The Illuminati's expression of Enlightenment ideas and their critique of traditional power did not disappear when the group was outlawed and destroyed. Indeed, their ideology then became more powerful, as democratic ideas began to spread across Europe. As Billington writes:

> Illuminist ideas influenced revolutionaries not just through left-wing proponents, but also through right-wing opponents. As the fears of the Right became the fascination of the Left, Illuminism gained a paradoxical posthumous influence far greater than it enjoyed as a living movement.[69]

The power of Enlightenment ideas, and the role these ideas played in fostering democratic revolution, suggest to us that the Order of the Illuminati was influential in shaping how we think about justifications for revolution, and about democracy. While conspiracy theorists suggest to us that the Illuminati masterminded a plan for world domination, historical evidence suggests the very opposite. In the shadow of a monarchical regime and in the context of a society dominated by tradition and the Church, Adam Weishaupt and his small and obscure band of German academics were instead one important element in spreading the Enlightenment ideas of freedom and equality.

What might be termed the real or documented positive histories of the Knights Templar, Freemasons, and Illuminati reveal that at the time of their existence, each of these groups was understood as problematic because it embodied changes that threatened the status quo. The Templars' innovation was the creation of the wealthy priest knight, a development that threatened both the Church and the French monarchy, and suggested the gradual transformation of European society. Power could, and eventually did, emerge from outside traditional strongholds. Freemasonry was an organization for the emerging industrial class, individuals who desired status, but advocated Enlightenment ideals, especially the notions of equality and brotherhood. The symbols of their ancient trade also neatly embody one of the foundations of modernity: the notion that it is possible to build a more perfect world. In this way, Masonic doctrines laid the foundation for democracy and troubled those who held power by virtue of heredity. Likewise, Baron Weishaupt and his Illuminati advocated for a world dominated by reason and science. Today, these principles seem innocuous, but in the 1700s, they were revolutionary: they suggest that human beings are equal, and in so doing, imply that only a political system that accounts for this equality can be justified. The Illuminati's ideology therefore threatened the aristocracy and the Catholic Church and its institutions.

Each in their own way, these groups were marked by the changing power structures in the societies from which they emerged. They were, in Wallace's terms, revitalization movements that eased the transformation from traditional to modern political life. For those who clung to old power structures, however, the new political horizon—and the groups that were concrete evidence of this impending change—were dangerous. Rather than embracing democracy and science, they argued that these ideas would destroy civilization.

In the 20th century, conspiracy theory resurfaced as a common way to talk about political life, and the Knights Templar, Freemasons, and Illuminati were an important part of that discourse. Much as they were perceived as evil in early and early modern Europe, they were likewise condemned in the 20th century. Once again, they were identified as threats to all that is good and right in the world. Nesta Webster argues in the interwar years that the aim of these organizations is to destroy British civilization, and when they appear in American political culture at the end of the 20th century, they are identified as a threat to Americans and American civilization. Rather than embodying the promise of democracy, they are a threat to it. In Britain and later the United States, the Knights Templar, Freemasons, and Illuminati became the repository of people's fears, and no longer are they viewed as being engaged in a limited conspiracy to simply change a country's leadership. Instead, conspiracy theories identify them as plotting to take over the world.

The next chapter of this book focuses on Nesta Webster, the person responsible for this change. In many ways, Webster was on the cutting edge of social change in Britain: she led a nontraditional life and was a vocal advocate for women's rights. Events in her life moved her, however, toward the political right, and eventually she became perhaps the most significant conspiracy theorist of the 20th century. Webster adapted the conspiratorial stories of the Knights Templar, Freemasons, and Illuminati to suit the context of a rapidly globalizing world and the conspiratorial architecture she developed remains the dominant way of conceptualizing conspiracies even in the 21st century. For Webster and those conspiracists that followed her, these conspiracy theories offer one place to rest their fears, while trying to maintain the status quo.

Chapter 3

From Conspiracy to Superconspiracy, from Europe to America: Nesta Webster and Modern Conspiracy Thinking

In the late 1700s, the political elite and the established Church were uncomfortable with the existence of secret societies to which they did not have access and over which they had no control. This was certainly true with respect to the Freemasons and the Illuminati. Both of these organizations embodied, in different ways, the major themes of modernity. As the previous chapter argues, the Masons' doctrine was, in its time, revolutionary. It asserted equality. Its foundation was the idea that one's station in life was not predetermined by birth; through hard work and education, individuals could transform their lives, and by extension, the world. To think in these terms is to imagine the possibility of democracy. Indeed, the foundation of the Masons' political views lie in a place most academics would find more acceptable than any Masonic publication: the writings of John Locke, and most particularly, his *Second Treatise on Government*.[1]

Locke writes that in the state of nature, all human beings are free and independent, and "that there cannot be supposed any such subordination among us, that may authorize us to destroy one another, as if we were made for one another's uses, as the inferior ranks of creatures are for our's."[2] In part for this reason, he contends:

> Men being, as has been said, by nature, all free, equal, and independent, no one can be put out of this estate, and subjected to the political power of another, without his own consent. The only way whereby any one divests himself of his natural liberty, and puts on the *bonds of civil society*, is by agreeing with other men to join and unite into a community for their comfortable, safe, and peaceable living one amongst another, in a secure enjoyment of their properties, and a greater security against any, that are not of it. This any number of men may do, because it injures not the freedom of the rest; they are left as they were in the liberty of the state of nature.[3]

Locke's arguments were echoed by—among others—Adam Weishaupt and the Illuminati. They advanced the ideas of the French Enlightenment and likewise advocated democratic revolution.

Seen in this light, it is perhaps not surprising that Europe's monarchies and the Church were concerned about secret societies. Indeed, Johnson goes so far as to suggest that in the years preceding the French Revolution, the elite's fear of the commoners was so pronounced that its members concocted stories of conspiratorial plots that endangered the world. He writes, "Many of the conservatives couldn't understand what—besides a satanic conspiracy—could be motivating the revolutionaries in their attacks on church and king."[4] Their fears were, of course, well-founded. In May of 1789, "absolute monarchy and aristocratic authority were overthrown forever in the most powerful kingdom in Christendom";[5] the French Revolution brought about a new era in human political history.

The real history of groups such as the Freemasons and Illuminati contrasts markedly with the elaborate mythologies fabricated by the elites of the late 1700s. Both organizations embodied and promoted the ideals of the Enlightenment, and despite their secrecy, were harbingers of democracy. The entrenched powers of the day, however, used them to their political advantage, suggesting that rather than freedom, these groups were in fact plotting to take control of the state. Likewise, advocates for democracy used the reverse argument to bolster their position; they blamed supposed Jesuit infiltration of secret societies for any setbacks in the achievement of their political agenda. In this environment then, conspiracy language was a tool of rhetoric, aimed against one's political enemies. How and why did such a simplistic political device become an explanation for all social, economic, and political events that so many people believe reasonable? Just as curiously, how did conspiracy thinking move from its home in Europe to America and find so many willing believers there? This chapter outlines the post–French Revolution path of conspiracy theory and examines in detail the pivotal role of the British author Nesta Webster in its development.

The European elites that dominated society and politics for centuries had rightly identified secret societies as a threat to their control and themselves used conspiracy theories as a means to shore up their power and forestall democracy. Their promotion of these theories was, however, sporadic, often contradictory, and rather ad hoc. As noted in chapter 2, over 50 books on the Illuminati—a veritable cottage industry—were published between 1784 and 1789. Weishaupt's careful strategy to supplement his organization's membership by engaging Freemasons also meant that Freemasonry was swept up in the controversy they created. Depending on whom you were speaking with, in both France and Prussia, these secret societies were accused of being both for and against the revolution, and of corrupting the revolutionary regime once it was in power. Indeed, publications such as the Marquis du Luchet's *Essai sur la secte des Illuminés* clearly illustrated that fear of conspiracy had spread not just across the national borders of Europe but also across its political spectrum. Luchet's work was interpreted by the French Enlightenment thinkers as providing evidence that the Illuminati and Freemasons were engaged in an anti-Enlightenment conspiracy. Alongside this book were publications such as Ernst von Göchhausen's *Enthüllung des Systems der Weltbürger-Republik* (1786), which contained stern warnings about the Enlightenment conspiracy that aimed to destroy the established religious and political order.[6] Notably, Göchhausen's book contains one of the first suggestions of what we know as the superconspiracies of today. In it, he argues that the Illuminati and Freemasons were in league to promote Enlightenment ideals, suggesting that the Illuminati were out to dominate Freemasonry as part of their larger plan to "emancipate all of mankind from religious and political slavery. Put specifically, to advance deism and cosmopolitanism."[7] In many ways then, the era that first generated the conspiracy theories so familiar to us today witnessed a situation similar to our own, albeit on a much smaller scale. Dozens of theories existed, and each one identified villains and victims in its own idiosyncratic arrangement. If you were a monarchist, the Illuminati and/or Freemasons and/or Knights Templar were plotting to overthrow all that was good and replace it with a secular dictatorship. If you were an advocate of democracy and the Enlightenment, then conservatives (frequently identified as the Jesuits) had infiltrated these same groups and were working to restore the monarchies of Europe and increase the power of the Church.

Then, as now, in a time of political upheaval and social uncertainty, conspiracy theories were a means to explain social change. They included sufficient references to reality to seem like reasonable explanations for what was happening, but they were by no means historical fact. Then, as now, they were a form of political argument, and the ongoing battle among them helped to ensure that the names of these organizations—one effectively a social club for the emerging middle class (the Freemasons) and one a disbanded organization of advocates for science and democracy (the Illuminati)—became ever more closely associated with political intrigue.

In this form, conspiracy theories continued to swirl around Europe and occasionally made their way to the United States. Johnson recounts the 1798 Illuminati Scare in New England, an uproar that once again involved conflict between political elitism and democracy. In 1797, John Robison, a professor of natural philosophy at the University of Edinburgh, published *Proofs of a Conspiracy against all the Religions and Governments of Europe*, a book that became popular on both sides of the Atlantic. Robison, whose academic specialization was in the sciences and whose previous claim to fame was his participation in Thomas Wolfe's expedition to Canada and the Battle of Quebec in 1759,[8] argued in the book that the Illuminati had infiltrated European Freemasonry and that these organizations were engaged in a plot to overthrow a number of European governments.[9] Robison's book was an instant success. Within a year, it was in its fourth English edition, and swiftly following that, it was translated and published in French, German, and Dutch.[10] Along with its French parallel, Abbé Barruel's *Memoirs of Jacobinism*, the conspiracy bug then crossed the Atlantic.

In the strongly religious communities of New England, Robison's and Barruel's books found a receptive audience. No less a figure than President Adams expressed concern about the apparent conspiracy of Illuminati and Freemasons, and Timothy Dwight, then president of Yale University, declared his concern in a sermon:

> [O]ur churches may become temples of reason…we may see the Bible cast into a bonfire, the vessels of the sacramental supper borne by an ass in public procession, and our children, either wheeled or terrified, uniting in the

mob, chanting mockeries against God, and hailing in the sounds of *Ca ira* the ruin of their religion, and the loss of their souls?...Shall we, my brethren, become partakers of these sins? Shall we introduce them into our government, our schools, our families? Shall our sons become the disciples of Voltaire, and the dragoons of Marat; or our daughters the concubines of the Illuminati?[11]

The language of conspiracy thus peppered the political debates that surrounded the Federalist debates. Much as it had been expressed in Europe, however, fears of conspiracy were not the weapon of just one side but were spread across the political spectrum. Both the Federalists and Anti-Federalists (notably Thomas Jefferson), as well as their respective followers, accused one another of being conspiracy sympathizers. By the end of it, Stauffer notes, "the word 'Illuminati' had lost all serious and exact significance and had become a term for politicians to conjure with."[12] Much as in Europe, accusations of conspiracy were used as political weapons.

Talk of political conspiracy had dominated American political discourse since the time of the American Revolution, when rebel leaders and their British counterparts accused one another of engaging in various plots. This situation was perhaps unavoidable in an environment where political rebellion was on everyone's mind. Strategy required secrecy. Scholars typically point to the revolutionary experience as a defining element of American political culture (in contrast to Canadian identity, which is linked to loyalty to the British crown.) David Brion Davis asks if it is possible "that the circumstances of the Revolution conditioned Americans to think of resistance to a dark subversive force as the essential ingredient to their national identity."[13] His point is supported by Knight, who agrees that this ongoing discussion of conspiracy might have become a permanent part of American identity:

> From the first encounters with the land and the people of the New World, the conspiratorial imagination of sinister forces has helped to constitute a sense of American national unity through a notion of *racial* identity. Early colonial scare stories of Indian cannibals conformed to classical moral cartographies....The typological radar of the Puritans likewise scanned their daily events and environment for clues to the deeper underlying plot of a Manichean struggle between savagery and civilization.[14]

The political philosopher George Grant characterized the Puritans' primal encounter with the North American continent as the "meeting of the alien and yet conquerable land with English speaking Protestants."[15]

Knight's analysis suggests, however, that the experience of revolution marks Grant's outward looking conqueror with a clear need to define "us" and "them." For him, conspiracy thinking is embedded in the forces that shape American identity, an influence that helps to explain the persistence of conspiracy theories in the modern era. Interestingly, Knight points out that globalization is likely a contributing factor in the current popularity of conspiracy theory. Americans must now define themselves and their community in the context of a globalized world, in which populations migrate quickly and diversity flourishes. This challenges their identity in a different way. Knight writes that the 21st century is "far more scary" because "we can no longer tell the difference between Them and Us."[16] Such a situation is ripe for a kind of free-floating anxiety about identity, and it might well help to explain the proliferation of modern conspiracy theories.

Although the roots of American conspiracy discourse are therefore deep, and some would say inescapable, their appearance in modern form is a relatively recent occurrence. For the Puritans and the 18th- and 19th-century Americans who followed them, real and imagined conspirators were limited in number and engaged in action with a limited and precise goal. Conspiracies might be identified as aimed at overthrowing a local council or plotting to steal from a neighbor. These kinds of illegal acts were small in scale, and the existence of conspirators and their conspiracies were usually empirically provable and dealt with by law enforcement agencies. This perception of conspiracy changed in the early years of the 20th century.

Lady Queenborough, an American socialite who is also known as Edith Starr Miller (1887–1933),[17] was perhaps partly responsible for this change. Author of a rather disorganized book of household hints entitled *Common Sense in the Kitchen*,[18] Starr also authored *Occult Theocrasy*, which was published in 1933, shortly after her death. In that book, she argues that Jews, leading a complex group of conspirators (including the Big Three and a wide-ranging variety of other organizations such as Sinn Fein and the American Civil Liberties Union), are attempting to control the world's political systems.[19] Queenborough's work was popular, but it was only a compendium of ideas already circulating among the American right. The book relies heavily on other authors' arguments and evidence. Its introduction, however, is particularly noteworthy, both in terms of its tone and content, which, save for some antiquated phrases, reads as if it could have been written today. Queenborough was concerned with what she viewed as rapid and unfortunate changes in society's morality and social structure.

She writes, "Today, most of the *good* people are afraid to be good! They strive to be broadminded and tolerant! It is fashionable to be tolerant—but mostly tolerant of evil—and this new code has reached the proportions of demanding intolerance of good. The wall of resistance to evil has thus been broken down and no longer affords protection to those who, persecuted by evil doers, stand in need of it."[20] Like earlier authors who were concerned about more limited conspiracies, Queenborough is afraid of changing social mores. Unseen forces are transforming the world she once knew:

> In these days when apparently vice triumphs and virtue must be penalized, it may be well for all of us to fight the undertow by which our children may be dragged under and must of necessity perish. Vice rings and secret societies form but one vortex into which youth is drawn and destroyed whilst the "good people", because of their ignorance, look on helplessly in despair....What must concern us all now is the protection of decency, or in other words— *Equal rights*—for such as are not vice adepts.[21]

In this new world, those who once held power are losing their authority to set the terms of political and social life. For Queenborough, those forces are, by definition, evil.

Queenborough met and married her husband in the United States, but after their wedding in 1921, they moved to Hertfordshire, England.[22] While in Britain, she participated in many of the far-right organizations of the day, including the British Fascisti and the British Union of Fascists. Her life therefore neatly intersected with that of the greatest conspiracy theorist of the 20th century, Nesta Helen Webster, and Queenborough studied Webster's work closely. Indeed, she was among the very first writers to develop and popularize Webster's ideas, which later were to be so popular in both the United Kingdom and the United States.

Interestingly, both Queenborough and Webster experienced the very particular conditions of life in interwar Britain from a similar place in society, and their lives were strikingly similar. Both were members of the upper classes; both were world travelers; and both were active in British far-right groups. In addition, both women married late, had daughters, and for their era, led somewhat unconventional lives. More importantly, however, in addition to their international travels, both experienced the social, political, and economic conditions of interwar Britain. In these spheres, the country was in a process of deep and profound upheaval. Immigration was beginning to alter the fabric of British society; women were mobilizing to achieve political rights; and Britain's empire and economic hegemony were beginning to dissolve.

In chapter 2, we considered how the beginnings of democracy and the emergence of scientific discourse moved those who were losing power and authority to explain that loss in conspiratorial terms. In the early 20th century, this process began again, first in the United Kingdom, and later, in America. Britain was once more at the center of a political change that in many ways can be considered the inevitable result of those first 18th-century steps toward democracy. While the 1700s brought democracy to male, property-owning Britons, the early to mid-20th century saw a more complete democratization of the nation. This process provoked debates concerning the rights of minority immigrants and minority religions, the political rights of women, and the rights of former colonies to self-government.[23] For the individuals and classes that until this time enjoyed the privilege of power, these debates and the resulting political change were not always understood as agents of positive transformation. Instead, they were experienced as a fundamental challenge to their position and Britain's role in the world. Indeed, like those in the 18th century who believed they ruled by moral right, the early 20th-century British elite likewise believed their social position, right to rule, and duty to civilize the world were responsibilities incumbent upon them.

Lady Queenborough argues in *Occult Theocrasy* that all secret societies: (1) have aims unfamiliar to the majority of their members; (2) have real power that is international in scope; and (3), and aim to concentrate "all political, economic and intellectual power into the hands of a small group of individuals, each of whom controls a branch of the International life, material and spiritual, of the world today."[24] Queenborough concludes that ultimately these secret societies are under the complete control of "Jewish financiers."[25] As Barkun notes, this assertion allowed her to link her theories to a wide range of anti-Semitic literature and filled in the many gaps in her argument and evidence.[26]

Despite its apparent originality, Queenborough's *Occult Theocrasy* was but a pale reflection of an earlier and more innovative text, and its impact in North America was limited. Nesta Helen Webster was the person most responsible for transforming conspiracy thinking and bringing modern conspiracy thinking to North America. In over a dozen books (including three novels), as well as hundreds of newspaper columns and political pamphlets, Webster set forth her innovative understanding of economics and politics, and her work remains influential—especially among conspiracy believers—today. Queenborough's work was simply a further explication of the ideas that Webster had developed in the preceding decade. The skewed logic of conspiracy thinkers, however, often sees Queenborough's *Occult Theocrasy* used as evidence that Webster's ideas are correct representations of history, and conversely, that Webster's writing is proof that Queenborough's arguments are correct. They are treated as two independent sources, both providing separate and original evidence that a particular conspiracy exists.[27]

Nesta Webster's experience of a Britain in the process of significant social upheaval moved her to question why and how such change could occur. In answering this question, she concluded that someone was making that change and therefore directing history. Webster's life and ideas are thus worth considering in detail, for they help to explain how particular social conditions might foster conspiracy thinking. Her role in the development and popularization of the superconspiracy theories so popular today also makes her a figure worthy of study. Her ideas are the foundation of modern conspiracy thinking, and today they are found in diverse places. Her analysis of world history is cited by conspiracy thinkers across the American right, for a multiplicity of purposes, and across the right-wing spectrum: from Pat Robertson (in his bestselling book, *The New World Order*)[28] to the blogs of Tea Party sympathizers[29] to the Militia and Patriot movements.[30] Conversely, the Islamic Party of Britain uses Webster's ideas to explain Napoleon's invasion of Egypt, the creation of Israel, and the fall of the Ottoman Empire, contending that the events of September 11, 2001, were part of a complex plan to destroy Islam, the last bulwark against Illuminism's subjugation of humanity.[31] Webster's work therefore shapes many individuals' understandings of politics, both in the United States and around the world.

From outside conspiracy discourse, the questions that emerge from these belief systems are not just puzzling, they are bizarre. Why do many Americans believe the Illuminati play a role in directing their nation's foreign policy in the Middle East? Why do some conspiracy believers see the Freemasons supporting Jewish plans for world domination, while others believe they are involved in an Islamic attempt to create one world government, and still others that they are aiming to destroy Islam? Bizarre as these questions are, even stranger is the fact that at least one part of the answer to them is found in Nesta Webster's early fascination with the love story of two aristocrats in prerevolutionary France. It is to Webster's life and ideas that we now turn.

Nesta Webster

Nesta Helen Bevan was born on August 14, 1876, at Trent Park, her family's estate in Hertfordshire, England. Her father was Robert Cooper Lee Bevan, a great-grandson of the founders of Barclay, Bevan, Tritton, and Co. (later Barclays Bank),[32] and her mother, Frances Shuttleworth, was the daughter of the bishop of Chichester. The Bevans were therefore wealthy, but Webster wrote in her autobiography that her father's religious beliefs—he had "devoted his life to the service of God"[33]—did not allow for luxury. She expressed the feeling, however, that her father, his religious faith, and his appreciation for the community were never fully appreciated by his banking colleagues. She was puzzled by this, for in her view, Barclays' success "was made…by the known integrity and good faith of the men who used the wealth it brought them *for the service of the community*" [emphasis added].[34] While many conspiracy theorists (including Queenborough) identify international finance as one component of attempts at world domination, this connection is not immediately apparent in Webster's work. Instead, she emphasizes the importance of wealth as a way to safeguard the British community. What one might take from this connection, however, is her implicit recognition of the way in which economic wealth was an essential component of that community's well-being. It suggests, too, that British Christianity is also somehow part of this equation.

When Nesta was 13, her father died, and the family home passed to her eldest half-brother; she therefore lived out the remainder of her youth in Europe, a period that she later described with all the regret the term implies, as an "exile" from Britain.[35] At the age of 17, she returned to England to finish her education. Her mother forbade her to attend Cambridge or Oxford (believing both institutions to be too liberal), and as a result, she attended Westfield College in Hampstead, where she initially entered a degree program in Classics and Mental and Moral Science. Frustrated by its required algebra courses, however, she eventually chose to continue her studies as a nondegree student, attending lectures in which she had an interest, primarily, as she records it, in English literature, Greek, and Mental and Moral Science.

Nesta left college in 1897 with only a partial degree. She turned 21 that year, and inherited her share of Robert Bevan's estate. Her reflection on that experience left her frustrated and unsure of what do with her life. She wrote:

> I had lived long enough now amongst women working for a purpose to despise an idle life and long to embark on some useful career. But what careers were open to women at that date? I might train to become a High School teacher like most of my college companions, but would it be right to take the bread out of the mouth of someone who needed it?[36]

Instead of immediately embarking on a career, she therefore opted instead to take an extended tour around the world that included Africa, India, Ceylon, Japan and Canada. In addition to the experience of world travel, Nesta recounts that this journey also fostered within her a respect for the world's many religion faiths, and she concluded that "behind all great religions there lies a central truth, which might be compared to a lamp with many coloured sides."[37] Her open-mindedness on the subject of religion was also reflected in the fact that she developed an ongoing interest in Buddhism, which led her to spend an extended period of time in Burma, a place she was "heartbroken" to leave.[38]

As a female member of the "educated class," Webster felt that she had only three career options: nurse, school teacher, or district visitor, and none of these appealed to her.[39] In 1903, she was still uncertain as to which career to follow but increasingly convinced that her true vocation was writing. In part to discover herself and her vocation, she then embarked on a second trip to Egypt, and an extended trip to Australia, Sri Lanka (then Ceylon), and India.[40] During the latter part of this trip she was introduced to Arthur Webster, a district superintendent of police. They were engaged within three weeks, and married on May 14, 1904. Nesta reports very few events between 1904 and 1914. As explanation, she comments that it may well be true that a happy woman has no history,[41] a remark that suggests that she had a developing feminist consciousness. During those years she gave birth to two daughters, Marjorie and Rosalind, and began her writing career.

Nesta's first novel, *The Sheep Track,* appeared in 1914 and chronicles the life of a young woman who leaves her sheltered home in Nice to travel to London to come out in society. Loosely autobiographical, it reflects her frustration at the limited opportunities open to women. The central character determines, however, that London society is a "sheep track." It is a world wherein "girls married amidst the applause of their friends to men they merely regarded as the inevitable accompaniment of substantial incomes…[a] system of pretended virtue."[42] In that world, to live according to one's own moral sense and convictions was tremendously difficult. Webster's heroine dabbles in "bohemian" society, eventually leaves London, and travels to Burma, Siam, and Japan. She concludes that it is not on the sheep track that the solutions to life's problems are to be found. The origins of Webster's title reveal the moral of her story. It is drawn directly from Seneca: *"Let us not, therefore, follow like sheep, but rather govern ourselves by reason than by other men's fashions"* [emphasis in original].[43]

The Sheep Track parallels Webster's own life: her sheltered existence in Cannes, her education and difficult experiences in London, and her decision to embark on extended world travel. Despite its popularity, the book is not particularly compelling reading for the modern reader. It does, however, condemn the nature of women's lives in early 20th-century society and forcefully argues that they should pursue meaningful careers. The novel received generally favorable reviews (the *New York Times* referred to it as "delightful"),[44] and within six months it was in its fourth printing. Webster clearly had a talent for writing.

In the autumn of 1914 she published her first overtly political tract, *Britain's Call to Arms, An Appeal to our Women.* In it, she calls on British women to encourage men to join the war effort. Webster argues that for every "one man who has answered the call to arms a dozen women have responded…needlework and nursing remain so far almost the only ways by which, at this critical hour, the great majority of women can…serve their country."[45] *Britain's Call to Arms* suggests that women are both more willing to serve their country in the war effort than men and more capable of understanding the implications of German victory, which would result in "an iron government such as they have never dreamt of,…all personal liberty would be done away with."[46] From her standpoint, it is therefore incumbent upon British women to make British men aware of the gravity of the situation and to rally them to action.

Webster's faith in women's political capabilities is echoed in a later article "Women and Civilisation" (1920). There she argues that men are wholly ignorant of women's true nature; the only type of women they know anything about, she writes, are "Primitive Women," who live to serve only the material needs of men and their offspring. Webster writes that these women, whose horizons are "entirely bounded" by men, do not seek their own individual development, and are therefore "inevitably the inferior" of men.[47] When women are left so "uneducated, uncultivated, unenlightened, [they are] too often the foolish, futile creature[s]"[48] that ignorant men believe all women to be. Webster suggests that women are best served when they are "cultivated," well-educated, and refined. She writes that in her experience, women's education is so different and inferior to that of men, and their life experiences so circumscribed, that it is impossible to know how great their minds and abilities might truly be. When this situation is rectified, she implies, women and men may well be true equals. Webster's conclusion of this argument is curious, and its significance appears in her later conspiracy writing. She concludes that the golden era of women's supremacy was prerevolutionary France, when powerful women never attempted to compete directly with men but instead drew strength from other areas where they excelled, in particular, "the power of organisation and the power of inspiration."[49] In this way, they extended a powerful influence over their society. In a repetition of her earlier argument in *Britain's Call to Arms*, the article closes with what is again a call for women's political action. Women's power, she writes, must be exerted in order to preserve "civilisation" in the postwar era.

Webster's work concerning women's rights reflects many of the themes and contradictions of her age. Her pleas for the recognition of women are in part an argument for women to exert a "civilizing influence" on society. At the same time, however, she calls upon them to abandon the life of the "primitive woman" and demands that all women receive a better education and greater opportunities. In her later writings, however, these themes are absent. She does not abandon these beliefs, but what is for her a greater cause takes precedence. An experience she had four years before writing *The Sheep Track* came to dominate her political agenda. Indeed, it marked the remainder of her life.

Webster proves false the assumption that all conspiracy theorists are of lower socioeconomic standing, poorly educated, and intolerant of difference (both cultural and religious).[50] She was a member of the British upper class, reasonably well-educated and well-traveled, and open-minded with respect to her religious faith. She even anticipated the late 20th-century Western fascination with Buddhism. In broad terms, she was also what could loosely be described as feminist in her outlook. At the same time, however, she was also increasingly uncomfortable with the profound social, economic, and political changes occurring in Britain, and she began to search for explanations as to why the world around her was in such a state of upheaval. An experience she had earlier in her life helped to answer that question.

In the winter of 1910, while she was living in Switzerland, Webster came across *Portraits de Grandes Dames,* a volume of essays by Imbert de Saint-Amand. Its discovery was pure chance. On a snowy day, she discovered it in the library of her hotel. The story of the Comtesse de Sabran and her lover, the Chevalier de Boufflers, aristocrats whose lives were entwined with the French Revolution, enthralled her. Upon her return to London, she acquired a compilation of their letters, *Correspondance de la Comtesse de Sabran et du Chevalier de Boufflers* (1875). Webster immersed herself in their story and became convinced that much of it was familiar to her. Eventually, she developed the sense that she had personally lived through the French Revolution. In light of this realization, she reflected on and reinterpreted much of her life. She wrote of the experience, "Now all the memories of my childhood came flooding back to me, the sense of apartness from the family circle in the old days at Trent, that first journey to Paris, the arrival at the Gare du Nord....Walking through the streets, especially in the Rue Saint-Honoré, I would say to myself, "I have seen these streets running with blood."[51] Webster's Buddhist leanings inclined her to believe that she was the reincarnation of a French aristocrat, and possibly even Madame de Sabran herself.[52] This inclination, a result of Webster's personal affection for Buddhism, and her choice of reading on a winter afternoon, became the motivating force for 20th-century conspiracy theory.

In 1916, Webster published *The Chevalier de Boufflers,* which recounted the Chevalier's and Madame Sabran's lengthy romance. The book received reasonable reviews and was popular with the general public: ultimately it was reprinted 15 times.[53] Indeed, the scholar Richard Thurlow suggests that the quality of Webster's early books suggest that she could have become "a fine popular historian," for her work evidences strong literary skills and a "meticulous attention to detail."[54] In researching this book, however, Webster came to the conclusion that most histories of the French Revolution were inaccurate. She therefore continued her study of the French Revolution through the last two years of the First World War, driven by what she characterized as an "impelling force" to present the truth to the world.[55] The result of that effort, *The French Revolution, A Study in Democracy* was published in 1920. The work embodies the coming together of her personal interest in the Revolution and her developing political ideology.

Nesta Webster's great empathy for the Chevalier de Boufflers and Madame Sabran extended to the French aristocracy as a whole, and reviewers commented on what they felt was her "unsympathetic attitude toward democracy," as well as her reliance on royalist and antirepublican sources.[56] Webster believed that the Revolution and democracy destroyed much of what was good in French society, and by the conclusion of her research, she had determined that it was impossible that the masses created such an upheaval themselves.[57] It was therefore reasonable to question "by whom was it made?"

The French Revolution, like many significant political events, was the result of a number of economic and political forces that aligned at a particular moment to yield change. In the case of the French Revolution, these forces included such factors as a series of European wars, French debt, taxation, food shortages and famine, and the emergence of ideology as an organizing force in political organization and activity. Webster, however, concluded that a conspiracy of secret societies had created it in order to further their plan to control the world. While she acknowledged there were specific conditions that might make the country ripe for a revolution, she argued that "kindling" the flame of revolution required the action of interested conspirators. In order to understand it, "we must examine the intrigues at work amongst the people; these and these alone explain the gigantic misunderstanding that arose between the King and his subjects, and that plunged the country on the brink of regeneration into the black abyss of anarchy."[58] Indeed, she concluded that the Illuminati's "dark design" was behind a multipronged conspiracy operating across many states that included four critical conspiracies, "the Orléaniste intrigue for a change of dynasty, the Prussian scheme for breaking the Franco-Austrian Alliance, the gradually evolved conception of a Republic, finally of a Socialist State…working for world revolution and the destruction of Christian civilization."[59]

The French Revolution was not entirely well received by the mainstream press. By the time of its publication, Webster was an established author, and her stature was such that her work was reviewed in both the popular press and academic journals. Critics attacked her royalist sympathies and her focus on conspiracies. In *The American Historical Review,* Fred Fling wrote that the book could have been written by Marie Antoinette had she "possessed the industry to accomplish the large amount of reading," and in the *American Political Science Review,* Sidney Fay commented that it "reads like an anti-bolshevist account of the Russian Revolution."[60]

By the time of *The French Revolution*'s publication, Webster was convinced that from the time of Baron Weishaupt, through the Illuminati and Freemasons, secret societies had influenced the direction of human history. Their power was now exerted through many agencies but particularly those on the political left. Internationally, Webster identified the Soviet Union, and Bolsheviks, as particular threats. This "alien conspiracy" had now invaded Britain, the "greatest stronghold of Christian Civilisation." Within the United Kingdom, efforts to unionize workers, the British Communist Party, and Sinn Fein (an organization she believed was directed by the "International Communist Movement") were working for revolution.[61]

In *World Revolution, The Plot Against Civilization* (1921), Webster continues this theme, writing that the world is in crisis, as evidenced by the spread of socialism and anarchism, and that her intent is to connect systematically secret societies' activities to the history of revolution.[62] She writes, "The revolution through which we are now passing is not local but universal, it is not political but social, and its causes must be sought not in popular discontent, but in a deep-laid conspiracy that uses the people to their own undoing."[63]

According to Webster, the origins of this conspiracy are in the link between Grand Orient Freemasonry with the Illuminati (recreated by Adam Weishaupt in 1776).[64] Webster claims that at meetings in 1782, the two organizations formed an association that undertook a "definite revolutionary campaign" aimed at transforming human societies. Their goals included the creation of general mayhem and the destruction of all governments and religion. Through this, human beings could regain "primitive liberty," an idealized state of existence that existed before the chains of civilization limited human behavior and potential. These organizations now work in secret, according to Webster, and animate some of the most influential political forces of the day, including "Bolshevism."

For Webster, the conspirators have the capacity to manipulate all those who are unaware of their scheme, for their powers are "terrible, unchanging, relentless, and wholly destructive ... [they are] the greatest menace that has ever confronted the human race."[65] In *World Revolution*, she therefore traces the history of secret societies from the French Revolution through the Russian Revolution; her aim is not just to educate British citizens but also to inspire them to protect their state. She closes the book by linking these themes and emphasizing Britain's special role, suggesting that "this little island of ours [may] finally stem the tide of World Revolution and save not only herself, but Christian civilization."[66] Included in this book is her complex "Chart of the World Revolution," which provides a graphic representation of the complex links that Webster argued existed (both secretly and in public) among secret societies and revolutionary movements of her age (see Figure 1). The complex web of connections reflects the profound change that Webster initiated in conspiracy thinking. Instead of individual agents working to achieve limited goals, she understood conspirators as working together to control the entire political world.

In 1924, Webster published what became her most influential work, *Secret Societies and Subversive Movements*. She remarks in the preface that she would prefer to return to her study of the French Revolution but implies that it is her duty to further elucidate the origins of the current "revolutionary movement" that is "gathering strength for an onslaught not only on Christianity, but on all social and moral order."[67] The majority of this book focuses on the early history of forces that Webster has identified elsewhere: Pan-Germanism, Freemasonry, and Illuminism. In this work, however, she also develops her arguments concerning the role of the Jewish people in this worldwide conspiracy.

Webster's assessment of the Jewish role in secret societies deserves particular attention, as it is an important element of her popularity among modern far-right political movements.[68] Throughout the book, Webster discusses the role of Jews in specific secret societies. In her concluding chapter, "The Jewish Peril," however, she draws these points together, stating that "the immense problem of the Jewish Power [is] perhaps the most important problem with which the modern world is confronted."[69] Webster argues that it is clear that the Cabala (a Jewish mystical doctrine) and other sources clearly indicate that "the hope for world-domination" is not an idea attributed to Jews by anti-Semites, "but a very real and essential part of their traditions."[70] Webster maintains that this tradition has developed since the time of Jesus; at its theological core, it is a desire to overthrow Christianity and Christian civilization. Jews have been effective, Webster notes, at utilizing secret societies for their own purposes. She writes, "The influence of the Jews in all the five great powers at work in the world—Grand Orient Masonry, Theosophy, Pan-Germanism, International Finance, and Social Revolution—is not a matter of surmise but of fact."[71] Likewise, she argues, they play a role in the world's "minor subversive movements": psychoanalysis, "degenerate art," the cinema world, and drug trafficking. According to Webster, their influence in British politics is also clear. They promote

Chart of the World Revolution

(Grey denotes the open revolutionary forces, black the hidden forces of the Secret Societies)

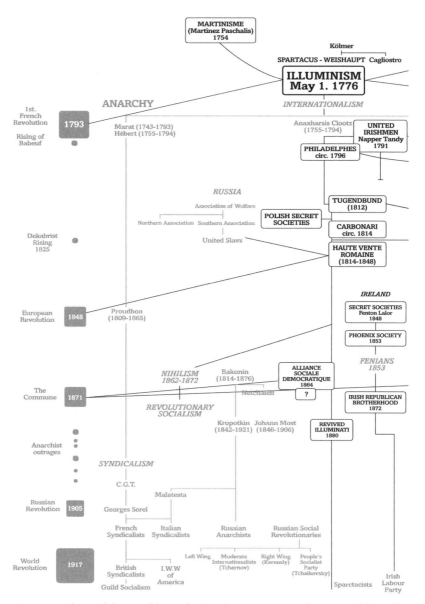

Figure 1: Chart of the World Revolution. (From Nesta Webster, *World Revolution, The Plot against Civilization* (London: Constable and Company, 1921).

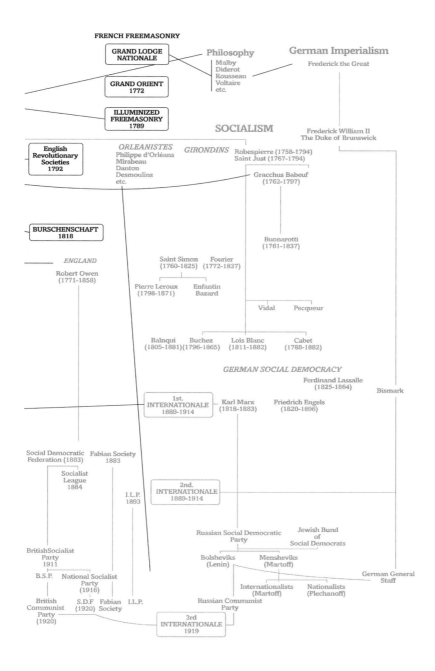

FRENCH FREEMASONRY

GRAND LODGE
NATIONALE

Philosophy
Malby
Diderot
Rousseau
Voltaire
etc.

German Imperialism
Frederick the Great

GRAND ORIENT
1772

ILLUMINIZED
FREEMASONRY
1789

SOCIALISM

Frederick William II
The Duke of Brunswick

English
Revolutionary
Societies
1792

ORLEANISTES
Philippe d'Orléans
Mirabeau
Danton
Desmoulins
etc.

GIRONDINS

Robespierre (1758-1794)
Saint Just (1767-1794)

Gracchus Babeuf
(1762-1797)

BURSCHENSCHAFT
1818

Buonarotti
(1761-1837)

ENGLAND

Robert Owen
(1771-1858)

Saint Simon   Fourier
(1760-1825) (1772-1837)

Pierre Leroux   Enfantin
(1798-1871)   Bazard

Vidal   Pecqueur

Balnqui   Buchez   Lois Blanc   Cabet
(1805-1881)(1796-1865) (1811-1882)   (1788-1882)

GERMAN SOCIAL DEMOCRACY

Ferdinand Lassalle
(1825-1864)

Bismark

1st.
INTERNATIONALE
1889-1914

Karl Marx
(1818-1883)

Friedrich Engels
(1820-1896)

Social Democratic
Federation (1883)

Fabian Society
1883

Socialist
League
1884

I.L.P.
1893

2nd.
INTERNATIONALE
1889-1914

Russian Social Democratic
Party

Jewish Bund
of
Social Democrats

British Socialist
Party
1911

Bolsheviks
(Lenin)

Mensheviks
(Martoff)

German General
Staff

B.S.P.   National Socialist
Party
(1916)

Internationalists
(Martoff)

Nationalists
(Plechanoff)

British
Communist
Party
(1920)

S.D.F   Fabian   I.L.P.
(1920) Society

Russian Communist
Party

3rd
INTERNATIONALE
1919

Bolshevism through the Labour Party, and although Conservatism (because of its patriotic traditions) has typically been free of Jewish influence, it was "precisely at a moment when Conservative organization had passed largely into Jewish hands that Conservatism met with the most astounding disaster in the whole of its history."[72] Webster concludes this chapter by noting that the real danger to Britain (and Christian civilization) springs from the unity of the Jewish people, "Far more potent than the sign of distress that summons Freemasons to each other's aid at moments of peril is the call of the blood that rallies the most divergent elements in Jewry to the defence of the Jewish cause."[73] Webster argues that it is this solidarity that is the real cause of anti-Semitism. Even if it might be true that the Jewish people are not the central force behind all secret societies, their threat comes at a moment when Britain and "Christian civilization" are being "systematically destroyed by the doctrines of International Socialism."[74] *Secret Societies and Subversive Movements* thus suggests that she believes that the Jewish people are an integral part of the conspiratorial forces that threaten civilization. Webster concludes that the only way to save Britain from this imminent destruction is through a "great national movement," much like Italian Fascism. It triumphed, she claims, because it was democratic and progressive, and appealed to the most noble human instincts, patriotism and self-sacrifice.[75]

Webster's theories about Jews and their role in secret societies fell on willing ears. As Holmes points out, while extremist anti-Semites were relatively rare, there existed a generalized low level of anti-Semitic sentiment in post–World War I Britain.[76] There is perhaps no better example of this than Winston Churchill's 1920 speech, "Zionism and Bolshevism," reprinted in the *Illustrated Sunday Herald.* Churchill addresses the issue of Jewish loyalty to Britain and identifies a "sinister confederacy" of internationalist Jews that was behind every subversive movement from the 19th century onward through the Russian Revolution, "From the days of Spartacus-Weishaupt to those of Karl Marx, and down to Trotsky (Russia), Bela Kim (Hungary), Rosa Luxembourg (Germany), and Emma Goldman (United States), this world-wide conspiracy for the overthrow of civilisation and for the reconstitution of society on the basis of arrested development, of envious malevolence, and impossible equality, has been steadily growing."[77] The speech, a curious combination of anti-Semitism and praise for Europe's Jewish population, advocates a homeland for Europe's Jewish population in Palestine. Churchill's source for this conspiratorial history and his political plan is none other than Nesta Webster, evidence not only of the widespread popularity of her ideas but also of her growing political influence.

The tremendous success of Webster's *Secret Societies* therefore helped to determine the future direction of the author's life. First, her conclusions moved her to become more directly politically active. Second, the book's success determined that despite her efforts to become a respectable historian of the French Revolution (and she published two more lengthy books on the topic), her lasting impact was to be as a conspiracy theorist. Indeed, the book's success made her a minor celebrity. She quickly became a recognized "authority" on secret societies, and with that status, became a frequent contributor to the right-wing newspaper *The Patriot*. She published columns and engaged in debates relating to various conspiracy theories, and the paper's editors publicized her books and public appearances.[78] Occasionally, she also published long-running series on conspiracy-related topics (for example, "Anti Revolutionary Organisation," which ran in seven parts, through January and early February of 1926). Her work was also frequently the subject of articles and commentary within the paper.

During this time, too, Webster also became politically active in the British Fascists Ltd., a movement that was not immediately concerned with Fascist ideology, but instead, focused its political program on the fear of a Communist uprising, a concern dear to Webster's heart.[79] In joining the Fascists, Webster was not unusual. Recent analyses make clear that the movement and its ideology were animated by women.[80] Her role was different, however, because she was politically prominent before she joined the movement. Indeed, some scholars speculate that Webster was drawn to the Fascist movement more as "a vehicle to disseminate her opinions rather than as a philosophy to be embraced."[81] In 1927, she became a member of its leadership, the Grand Council, and during her tenure spoke at their public meetings and wrote articles for the group's publications, the *Fascist Bulletin* and the *British Lion*.[82] The British Fascists afforded Webster increased political visibility, but she abandoned the party in mid-1927 and instead embarked upon her own, related political project, which she called "The Patriots' Inquiry Centre."[83]

Webster believed that Communism was making inroads in British society, and as evidence, she cited the fact that the Labour Party appeared to be strengthening its hold on the lower classes. Although it had officially repudiated Communism, Webster believed this move was superficial and intended to placate concerned Britons. She argued that the party admitted

Communists through its support of Trade Unionists. In an effort to counter their influence, she proposed a "bureau of information" that would serve as a clearing house for all workers in the "anti-Socialist cause," and she offered her own collection of research as a starting point for the Centre's library. In October of 1927 she first advertised the Centre in *The Patriot.* Although she noted that the financial support of "a few patriotic persons" had been obtained, and an office in central London secured, she also asked for further financial contributions. The Centre would contribute to the anti-Communist cause through coordinating the work of organizations and individuals "in every part of the world."[84]

As Markku Ruotsila points out, the Patriots Inquiry Centre was effectively an agency for anti-Socialist and anti-Semitic speakers.[85] In addition, its mission was shaped by an underlying conviction that it was essential to defend and propagate Christianity. These endeavors would sustain the battle against the conspirators. The Patriots' Inquiry Centre was a viable operation for a number of years, but evidence of its activities disappeared from the pages of *The Patriot* early in the 1930s. So too did original articles by Webster (although she did contribute a four-part series, "The Past History of World Revolution") in 1932. It was not until the late 1940s that she wrote for *The Patriot* again (a seven-part series, "Where Are We Going?," which focused on socialism and the threat it posed to Great Britain).[86] Gauging by the number and variety of her publications, Webster appears to have abandoned practical politics to once again pursue a full-time writing career.

During the 1930s, she published four books. *The Surrender of an Empire* continued her campaign to warn Britons of the various conspiracies that threatened the state while *The Secret of the Zodiac,* written under the pseudonym Julian Sterne, was a deliberate work of fiction. By now a well-known conspiracy theorist, Webster perhaps chose this pseudonym to suggest that the book was authored by a Jewish man who would have an insider's knowledge of the world conspiracy; the name Sterne is also a composite of the last four letters of Webster and the first two letters of Nesta. It told the story of "sinister unseen forces" that aimed to undermine civilization. Indeed, it is almost a summation of all the conspiracy theories she had suggested in her nonfiction works, mixed with suggestions about the occult. One of the characters in the book remarks, for example:

> I do think it possible that there have been and still are people who have in
> some way mastered the art of projecting thought and floating ideas in a way

unknown to the rest of the world...the political side of the movement is run on the same lines as the occult side, that is to say, on the old secret society system. The Communist Party in each country is in reality a secret society—few members know who are the real heads or where the direction comes from...in the secret communications of leading Communists...the phraseology used is absolutely that of the secret conspirators known as the Illuminati.[87]

To this mix, Webster even manages to throw in the French Revolution and suggest that the Communists intend to copy the French Republican calendar.[88] Although entertaining as a curiosity, the book is of dubious value as literature. Like her other conspiracy-related works, however, it remains in print.

Webster's two other major publications of the decade in fact marked a return to her other favorite topic, the French Revolution. *Louis XVI and Marie Antoinette, Before the Revolution,* and *Louis XVI and Marie Antoinette, During the Revolution* were lengthy tomes published within a year of each other in 1936 and 1937, respectively.[89] These works presented a sympathetic picture of the French monarch and Marie Antoinette, combined with Webster's argument that the French Revolution was devised and carried out by the Freemasons. The books were widely reviewed, and most commentators criticized Webster's argument but praised her skills as an historian.[90]

Webster's final pre–World War II political publication was a revised reprint of a series of articles she wrote for *The Patriot,* "Germany and England" (1938). The lengthy pamphlet criticized Britain's response to events in Europe, and it argued that Nazism was not as great a threat to Britain as "Bolshevism." Webster argued that Hitler's emphasis on "the superiority of the German race" was "only logical, since the essence of Fascismo and Nazi-ism is Nationalism, whilst that of Bolshevism is Internationalism."[91] Webster therefore argued that Britain should not fear Hitler or Nazism. Indeed, she argues:

In his strictures on pre-Nazi Germany, Hitler is undeniably justified; it was a matter of common knowledge just before and after the War that Berlin became a centre of iniquity, its night life worse in some respects than that of Paris; vice of an unspeakable kind was flaunted with impunity, nude midnight orgies took place in the West End of the city...

Whether Hitler is right in attributing all this to the Jews we cannot tell; there are depraved elements of every nation which need no inciting to vice. The fact remains, however, that since Hitler started to purge town life in

Germany, pornographic books and pictures have disappeared from the shops, the Youth movements have become clean and healthy, the cult of nudity has been suppressed. And all this has coincided with the expulsion or voluntary departure of a number of Jews from Germany.[92]

Webster does argue that she is "no blind admirer of Hitler," complaining that like most Britons, she prefers a regime of greater freedom. In addition, she argues that his policies have had a generally detrimental effect on Britain and have in some ways expanded the power of the worldwide conspirators. She writes, Hitler is:

driving out the Communists and Jews into other countries in such a way to enlist sympathy for them, instead of keeping them humanely under control in his own, he disregards the fact that he is helping to spread Bolshevism abroad and actually to strengthen the Jewish power.[93]

It is not Hitler who threatens Britain but instead the grand conspiracy that poses the most serious danger to Britain. Indeed, just as Churchill argued nearly 20 years earlier, Webster concludes that "the Jewish problem" could best be solved by creating a homeland for the Jews in "the vast unpeopled spaces of Soviet Russia," and that the "fabulous wealth of rich Jews all over the world could be used to settle them there."[94] For Webster, the cloud of war hanging over England is one that can easily be lifted. It requires recognition that war might bring about the end of civilization and that the real threat to Britain are the alien forces of the conspiracy.

Webster published much less frequently following the outbreak of World War II. Because the details of the final two decades of her life are largely unknown, however, it is difficult to assess whether personal reasons were responsible for this decline in output (in the spring of 1942, her husband, Arthur Webster, died),[95] or whether Hitler's role in World War II prompted her to revise her views on Fascism. She wrote a limited number of articles for *The Patriot* until its demise in 1950 and following that published only her final book, the autobiography *Spacious Days* (1950). Nesta Webster died in May of 1960.[96]

Webster wrote during a period of intense social and political change in Great Britain, and it is these types of eras that most typically produce conspiracy theory. Individuals are driven to explain the upheaval that surrounds them. As Moscovici writes, conspiracy theories are an attempt to integrate "one's image of society in one cause."[97] They are one way of eliminating cognitive dissonance, a situation where personal beliefs and reality conflict. A conspiracy theory allows one's own interpretation of the world to remain intact, and not require fundamental shift, when all threats to it are explained by a single omnipresent force.

Nesta Webster was threatened by challenges to the British Empire and its social hierarchy. Although her beliefs about the capabilities of women and her own political activism were nontraditional—and would have been appropriate for a more modern Britain—she was primarily concerned about the preservation of traditional society. As a result, she neglected her more feminist beliefs in order to pursue what she believed was a greater cause: warning the world of the conspiracy that threatened British civilization. Thus, like women of the left who participate in activism for a larger cause (for example, nationalist movements),[98] Webster chose to put her feminism second.

Three major themes dominate Webster's life and work: the desire to protect British civilization (as she defined it), the fear of those who threatened British civilization, and the conviction that forces beyond the control of average citizens control politics and its outcomes. For Webster, these beliefs helped provide an explanation for the political change that occurred during her lifetime.

Webster's assessment of the 20th-century political landscape, however, moved her to reconceptualize how people thought about conspiracy. It was evident to her that the relevant political world extended far beyond the borders of the United Kingdom. She realized, indeed celebrated, Britain's colonization of Africa and Asia; she believed that it was part of her country's mission to bring Christian civilization to the world. At the same time, however, that realization also expanded the range of Britain's enemies, and therefore the legion of conspirators who were working against her country and its purposes.

In some ways, Webster's conceptualization was visionary. The scholarly discipline of international relations did not begin in its modern form until the publication of E. H. Carr's *The Twenty Years' Crisis* in the mid-1930s. She realized the significance of a globalized world before many scholars. For Webster, however, that international world was clearly divided between the forces of good and the forces of evil, which were in conflict in a multitude of ways and places around the globe. From this perspective, it no longer made sense to talk about a single conspiracy. Taking a page from Adam

Weishaupt, she argued that there may be some evil force directing the plan but that its will was expressed in diverse ways. She argued that there were therefore invisible links between a multitude of different (and in her view sometimes superficially opposed) organizations who were all working toward the same purpose. In short, the conspiracy was everywhere.

Webster's reformulation of conspiracy theory was revolutionary. In response to a globalizing political environment, she transformed how conspiracy thinkers understood the world. In some ways, her innovations were inevitable. In an era where events occurring on the other side of the globe can affect our daily lives, conspiracy theory was destined to likewise expand. It was Nesta Webster who first effected this revolutionary change in conspiracy thinking. She created the first superconspiracy theory. It is small wonder that in the world of conspiracists, her work remains so popular today.

Chapter 4

Conspiracy in America?

In 18th-century Europe, traditional elites used the rhetoric of conspiracy theory in an attempt to stem the advancement of democracy and the spread of scientific discourse; these developments threatened their power. In the early 20th century, amateur historian Nesta Webster, moved by French aristocrats' resistance to the Revolution, and writing from her privileged position in British society, also embraced a conspiratorial understanding of history. Like those who first adopted conspiratorial thinking, Webster was concerned about social change that threatened her political community and her place in society. Webster, however, did not perceive conspiracies as a limited political strategy. Instead, as global power shifted away from Britain and toward America, Webster saw conspiracy everywhere, working through every possible facet of human existence. It aimed first to undermine British civilization and then would move on to an international agenda aimed at controlling the world. In this way of thinking, Webster fundamentally changed the nature of conspiracy theory. While future arguments would still be made that single-aim conspiracies existed, her work—linking numerous groups and plots in an international plan for control of human existence—allowed a whole new world of conspiracy thinking to develop.

As we will see, particular social, economic, and political conditions are conducive to the emergence of conspiracy theory in public discourse. These conditions existed at the emergence of conspiracy thinking, the interwar years, where they had a most direct effect on Britain, and at the close of the 20th century, when their impact was felt most clearly in the United States. Whether or not we are immediately aware of it, the condition of international politics and economics affects not just our day-to-day lives but also our perspective on the world. The most intense periods of upheaval and change occur when the powerful states that dominate world politics experience transformations in their abilities. In these times, conspiratorial thinking is most popular. The story of how and why conspiracism, and in particular superconspiracy theories, became so popular in the late 20th century United States is in part, therefore, the story of how global political power shifted during the past 100 years. To understand how and why this is so, we can look at similar changes that happened in Britain, which saw its global domination effectively conclude with World War II. For this reason, it is important to begin with a brief consideration of the history of international politics.

Scholars approach the study of international relations from a variety of perspectives; their field is multidimensional and they must account for not just individual interests (sometimes leaders are important) or state interests (sometimes a single state can engage in behaviors that have an impact on other states) but also the dynamics of the international system itself. Each level of analysis provides a different picture of international relations. One way of understanding how global politics works is to focus on its long history, and in particular, to examine the role of the world's truly great powers in shaping the international system of their day. International relations scholars have again many ways of undertaking this type analysis. Some focus on politics, some on economics, some on wars, and others attempt to combine all of these factors in their models. In his analysis of international relations, George Modelski argues that one can find patterns in the history of world politics. Specifically, he points out that global history can be understood as a series of nation-states responding to global problems with political, economic, and social innovations that allow them to reshape the world system.[1] This analysis supports the general idea of Western world history with which most individuals are familiar. Portugal dominated the system from the 1400s until the late 1500s, when the Dutch Republic came to lead it. Britain began its first era of domination with an alliance with the Dutch and, through a skillful use of political and military means, effectively institutionalized the Balance of Power system. Its defeat of Napoleon saw it rise to lead the system a second time, during which, Modelski argues, Britain's authority was supported by its economic power, a supremacy sustained by its position as the center of the industrial revolution.[2] World Wars I and II saw the decline of Britain and the emergence of the United States as a global leader.

Modelski argues that the United States adopted the same form of political leadership as had Britain. While many might point to the size and

power of the American economy as critical to its ascendancy as world superpower, Modelski suggests that it was not so much its massive economy
that achieved and maintained U.S. dominance, but instead, the quality of
the innovations within that economy. He writes that it was

> the kind of innovations it sprouted (such as the telephone, or the film in-
> dustry), the scope and quality of its science, and range and creativity of its
> media that helped to illuminate not only America but soon the entire world
> system. The science/knowledge revolution that followed clarified the nature
> of our world, laid the foundation for wholly upgraded ways of dealing with
> its problems, political and structural, and placed the quality of global order
> squarely on the world's agenda.[3]

Modelski's analysis of the international system thus points to the importance of the world's major powers in establishing global order. It also suggests how a power's dominance is comprised of a variety of factors, not just
military might. His assessment of system change, however, is that major
global wars have (so far) been the vehicle through which systemic change
is effected.

Modelski is concerned with illustrating the very existence of what he
calls "long cycles," and his evidence is compelling. His framework identifies long periods of stability, followed by periods of change and instability.
Notably, conspiracy theories increase in popularity during the periods of
time immediately before systemic change occurs. This suggests, perhaps, a
generalized uncertainty that might move individuals to look for new forms
of political explanation. Why does that uncertainty occur? Another long-
cycle analysis can help to explain how and why such deeply felt uncertainty
can exist in these time frames.

In his classic examination of the history of world politics, Immanuel
Wallerstein considers what it is that makes the world's superpowers so
dominant. He argues that continued jostling among the world's strong
states occurs continually but that there are periods of time in which one
state achieves a meaningful dominance, a situation that he refers to as hegemony.[4] Wallerstein argues that the military power and authority of each
hegemon (again, as Modelski suggests, the United Provinces, Great Britain,
and the United States, in sequence) is supported by its material capabilities.
The economy of each of these great powers first achieves dominance in ag-
riculture and industry, then in commerce, and finally in finance. Wallerstein

argues, however, that the amount of time that each power dominates in all three spheres is limited, and it is only when that dominance exists in all three sectors that real hegemony exists, and that this situation that is "rare and unstable."[5] The specificity of his model means that his dates differ slightly from Modelski's assessment; Wallerstein concludes that hegemony for the United Provinces existed from 1620 to 1672, for Great Britain from 1815 to 1873, and for the United States from 1945 to 1967. During the long period of hegemonic decline that precedes a system-altering war, the dominant state will experience instability and, in sequence, a loss of power in each of those three economic sectors, first in agro-industrial production, then in commerce, and then in finance.[6]

Wallerstein is interested in assessing the interrelationship of economic power and the politics of the international system, a concern of only marginal interest to us here. His analysis illustrates, however, that long before a hegemon loses its authority in the inevitable war that marks the end of its reign (a conflict that is in part a result of its fading power), it suffers political and economic uncertainty. Its authority declines; its economy weakens; and it can no longer obtain optimum political outcomes. As each particular economic sector loses its advantage, it suffers instability and decline. These disruptions have both a political and an economic impact.

Despite their differences, both Modelski and Wallerstein suggest that international politics has a type of cyclical pattern: major wars produce new hegemons, which through economic and technical innovation lead the international system for a period of time. Inevitably, however, hegemonic superpowers decline. Military overextension and/or economic competition wear them down. They are less able to sustain rules of the international system that support their political dominance and economic growth, and less often the site of technical innovation. They are therefore more likely to lose the advantages they have over their competitors. This leads to a period of instability, which then results in conflict, and the cycle begins again. Modelski's and Wallerstein's analyses therefore make clear what people living through these periods of change perhaps sense only in a very general way: the entire structure of the international system is shifting, and that transformation has an impact not just on the ways that states interact but also on individual lives. A destabilized economy is not just important for a nation's balance of payments. It also threatens job security and personal well-being. A loss of political power and the threat of war likewise mark a nation's population. Living with such profound uncertainty is not easy.

Modelski, Wallerstein, and many other international relations scholars[7] suggest to us that with a reasonable degree of certainty and accuracy, one can point to periods of notable instability in the international state system: the late 1700s, interwar Britain, and the late 20th century. One can also identify time periods wherein conspiracy theories became a particularly popular form of political discourse: at the emergence of the Illuminati scare in the late 1700s, in the popularity of Nesta Webster's work in 1920s Britain, and in American political discourse, from roughly the early 1990s until the present day. These periods overlap. In the late 1700s, conspiracy thinking was rampant across the European continent. As hegemonic power shifted toward Britain, so too did the power of traditional, hereditary elites shift toward the people, and Europe's fledgling democracies were born. These changes transformed the Western world. Those who were left behind, who lost their privilege, wealth, and power, sometimes chose to blame a conspiracy.

Through World War I, the interwar period, and World War II, global hegemony continued to shift from Great Britain to the United States. The aristocracy struggled to maintain its "deep nostalgic vision of Empire,"[8] sustained by its view of Britain as the epitome of civilization, but the political and economic strengths that had supported those national myths of identity ebbed away. As Andrew Marr writes:

> Britain had arrived blinking into a new world still cloaked in the archaic nineteenth-century grandeur of imperialism. The Americans were busy creating their own commercial empire, moving into markets vacated by defeated or exhausted rivals. The Soviet Union was equally busy extending its political empire, funding local dictators and occasionally lurching towards more dramatic confrontation....Against these new empires, the moth-eaten pretensions of a mild mannered king-emperor, a few battleships and a modest number of colonial governors in baggy shorts barely seemed relevant.[9]

From their privileged positions, Nesta Webster and Lady Queenborough understood this transformation as a threat to British civilization, although in retrospect it can be viewed as simply the decline of British material power. As she wrote in the conclusion of *Secret Societies and Subversive Movements*:

> Those of us who, sacrificing popularity and monetary gain, dare to speak out on this question have not hatred in our hearts, but only love for our country. We believe that not only our national security but our great national

traditions are at stake, and that unless England awakens in time she will pass under alien domination and her influence as the stronghold of Christian civilization will be lost to the world.[10]

Like the 17th-century European elite who were convinced the Illuminati were out to destroy them, Webster saw conspiracy behind the changes in Britain. In the context of an expanding international community, she expanded conspiracy theory too. While single agents might engage in nefarious activity for the limited purpose of controlling a government, they were part of a larger plan. Under the direction of a single force, secret societies around the world were linked together, and their goal was not just to destroy British civilization but to control the world.

Through the 1920s, Webster was increasingly concerned with what she first calls simply "Socialism" (in 1921's *World Revolution*), and later refers to more frequently as "International Socialism" (in *Secret Societies and Subversive Movements,* 1924).[11] For Webster, socialism is "essentially a system of deception devised by middle-class theorists and in no sense a popular creed."[12] Neither is it an independent movement with its own specific political goals. Instead, it is a tool of Illuminized Freemasonry:

> [T]he world-revolution is not only founded on the doctrines of illuminized Freemasonry, but has adopted the same method of organization. Thus, after the plan of the Batinis onward, we shall find the forces of revolution divided into successive grades—the lowest consisting of the revolutionary proletariat, the *chair á revolution* as Marx expressed it, knowing nothing of the theory of Socialism, still less of the real aims of the leaders; above this the semi-initiates, the doctrinaires of Socialism, comprising doubtless many sincere enthusiasts; but above these again further grades leading up to the real initiates, who alone know wither the whole movement is tending.[13]

Webster's deep concern about the spread of International Socialism and its real goals are interesting in and of themselves, for they reflect many of the themes that have been discussed here. She asserts that socialism is not what it seems, that it is rooted in Illuminati ideology, and that like the Illuminati of old, modern Socialists are unaware of the real goals of their movement. Its goal is not the creation of Socialism or even Communism, but instead, "a moral and spiritual revolution" that will destroy all human advancement, and obliterate the Christian ideal.[14] Interestingly, she makes no meaningful connection to America's rising power. In Webster's view, of course, Great Britain was the bastion of Western civilization. She was troubled by the increasing diversity of Britain's population, and specifically, by increased Jewish immigration from the European continent, and worried about Britain's loss of international influence.

As Modelski and Wallerstein make clear, ultimately, Britain's ability to dominate international politics and economics declined. Contrary to Nesta Webster's expectations, however, Christianity and Western society survived. The bipolar state system that emerged following World War II proved to be a particularly fertile ground for Webster's conspiracy theories to take root. Although her ideas were based on a conceptualization of Britain and its culture as the center of resistance to the conspirators, for all of the reasons discussed above, her arguments proved remarkably portable.

Chapter 1 examined how conspiracy theories facilitate the development of a dualistic worldview. Their assessment of reality clearly identifies good and evil, and leaves no room for ambiguity. As the world's post-1945 states divided themselves into two major alliances and political leaders' apocalyptic language ratcheted up the tension between the United States and the Union of Soviet Socialist Republics (USSR), conspiracy thinking found a new home. Nuclear weapons and the tension between the United States and the USSR served to make the Cold War environment one of great and pervasive political dread. As William Faulkner described this sense of terror in his Nobel Prize acceptance speech, "Our tragedy today is a general and universal physical fear so long sustained by now that we can even bear it. There are no longer problems of the spirit. There is only the question: When will I be blown up?"[15] In the 1950s, Senator Joseph McCarthy engaged in such a vigorous and wide-ranging witch hunt for Soviet power in the United States that Richard Fried wrote that McCarthy "personified the search for Communist influence throughout American life."[16] Fear marked American political discourse.

With the benefit of hindsight, many international relations scholars now argue that the United States was in fact the emerging hegemon in this period, an analysis they support with reference to the nature of its alliances and its clear advantages in the economic sphere. At the time, however, the United States' eventual domination was far from certain. Indeed, to some Americans, the Soviets and their brand of Communism seemed to be winning the day. In the United States, one way of understanding this uncertainty was to interpret the Soviets' pursuit of power as part of a larger conspiracy, and their tactics as likewise conspiratorial in nature.

Robert Welch, founder of the John Birch Society (an organization whose stated aim was to "promote less government, more responsibility, and a better world"[17]), promulgated what proved to be one of the most long-lasting and influential of these conspiracy theories. His ideas are particularly worth noting because they clearly evidence the change to conspiracy architecture that Nesta Webster popularized. Welch's ideas, however, are conditioned by the new international political landscape and the specific political community in which he lived.

Robert Welch wrote in the John Birch Society's *Blue Book* that the Soviets were succeeding in spreading Communism around the globe, having obtained Eastern Europe, gained a foothold in Asia, encircled Western Europe, and conquered a number of South and Central American countries.[18] The United States was the last bastion of freedom, and it too was in peril. While it willingly gave up its sovereignty to various international organizations (including the United Nations), the Communists were covertly gaining control of those same organizations, in Welch's words, "[O]ne day we shall gradually realize that we are already just a part of a world-wide government ruled by the Kremlin."[19] At the same time, Welch maintained, the Communists were infiltrating the United States itself, having realized the strategic benefit of fomenting civil war, compared to an international war with an external enemy. As evidence of this plan, Welch argued that the political and social unrest in the American South was due to the Communists' intervention in that region. He wrote:

> The trouble in our southern states has been fomented almost entirely by the Communists for this purpose. It has been their plan, gradually carried out over a long period with meticulous cunning, to stir up such bitterness between whites and blacks in the South that small flames of civil disorder would inevitably result. They could then fan and coalesce these little flames into one great conflagration of civil war, in time, if the need arose. The whole slogan of "civil rights," as used to make trouble in the South today, is an exact parallel to the slogan of "agrarian reform" which they used in China.[20]

Welch interpreted social change neither as a positive development for African Americans, nor as a move toward a United States that more accurately reflected the constitutional principles of equality and freedom. Instead, progress toward a more just and equitable political community is understood to be the result of a Communist conspiracy. His assessment of African Americans' struggle for civil rights as an instrument for Communist domination of American politics fits well within the argument made here. Changes to the international system and political developments within the United States provoked what Hofstadter referred to as a "political paranoia."

In terms of the development of conspiracy thinking in the United States, Welch's interpretation is important for several reasons. Most notably, he popularized Nesta Webster's ideas in America. As Michael Barkun notes, Gerald Winrod (an anti-Semitic Kansas preacher and outspoken advocate of the *Protocols of the Elders of Zion*) first brought Webster's ideas to the United States in his 1935 pamphlet "Adam Weishaupt, a Human Devil."[21] In addition, Revilo Oliver, a white supremacist Holocaust denier,[22] publicized Webster's work (referring to her as "the courageous and scholarly Mrs. Nesta Webster"[23]), and evidence suggests that he even corresponded with her. Likewise, Oliver was a founding member of the John Birch Society, and it is likely that Oliver brought Webster's work to the attention of Robert Welch.[24] Both Winrod and Oliver were particularly concerned with potential Soviet conspiracies to harm America, but at the same time, they were also clearly associated with anti-Semitic extremism. Winrod, for example, argued that the Illuminati and the Jews were "the direct instruments of Satan on earth,"[25] and Oliver went so far as to assert that the vaporization of the earth's Jews was a "beatific vision."[26] If references to Webster's work had been limited to their publications, her influence might not be so widespread. Welch, however, was not tarnished by this anti-Semitism, and as noted above, the John Birch Society had if not a widespread appeal, a more mainstream audience than both Winrod and Oliver.

Welch's view was that the threat to America and the world was not simply Soviet power but what he termed a Communist conspiracy. Evidence of the conspiracy existed outside government institutions, both nationally and internationally:

> [I]ts tentacles now reach into all of the legislative halls, all of the union labor meetings, a majority of the religious gatherings, and most of the schools *of the whole world* [emphasis in original]. It has a central nervous system which can make its tentacles in the labor unions of Bolivia, in the farmers' cooperatives of Saskatchewan, in the caucuses of the Social Democrats of West Germany, and in the class rooms of the Yale Law School, all retract or reach forward simultaneously.[27]

Welch intones Americans to be suspicious of their own government and the social institutions that help to sustain it. Notably, too, he adopts Nesta Webster's contribution to conspiracy thinking. Traditional conspiracy thinking focused on a single conspiracy with a single goal. Welch follows Webster's conceptualization of international conspiracies in that he argues both that the conspiracy functions through many groups simultaneously and that its goal is to attain complete world domination.

In addition, much as Nesta Webster emphasized Britain's role in preserving Christian civilization and democracy, Welch emphasizes America's exceptionalism. Many states had already fallen victim to Communism and the ideology of collectivism, but the American spirit of individualism may defeat the conspiracy's power. The United States is, Welch argues, "the seat of a whole new civilization," "fiercely proud of its differences from Europe, and of its indigenously vigorous customs, culture, and destiny."[28]

These ideas—the pervasiveness of the conspiracy, its ultimate goal, and America's role in defeating it—helped Welch's conceptualization of the conspiracy to take root in American political discourse, and its capacity to inspire believers sustained his organization, the John Birch Society. The structure of Welch's belief system bears a remarkable similarity to that of Nesta Webster. Notably, both authors published their most influential works during periods of deep structural change in the international system. Welch, however, wrote as the United States ascended to international hegemony, a transformation that, although destabilizing, promised international political recognition and an expanding and innovating economy. His ideas emerged in an ideological environment conditioned by years of Senator McCarthy's witch hunt for Communists (as well as other anti-Communist publications), and they took hold immediately.

The Birch Society membership was relatively small; at its peak it may have had as many as 100,000 members, but scholars suggest that its numbers were likely significantly smaller, with perhaps as few as 30,000 active participants in the mid-1960s.[29] Stone's analysis of the organization's membership is worth noting. Her findings suggest that in this time frame, the Society's membership could be characterized as "well-educated, reasonably young individuals with substantial family incomes...[and] upper-status occupations."[30] Indeed, Stone argues that members are not those suffering economic deprivation but instead individuals who are disillusioned by "the social, political, and moral climate of America...[and] feel threatened by the uncertainties of their world, with its rising taxes and inflation, its civil turmoil, and its international instability."[31]

In part for these reasons, Westin suggests that despite its relatively small size, the Birch Society became the most attractive American right-wing organization since the 1930s.[32] Its upper-middle-class members were drawn to its special place in the ideological sphere, "between the 'hate' right and the semi-respectable right."[33] Public-opinion polls of the day suggest that over 56 million Americans were familiar with the Birch Society (even Gallup noted its "extraordinary" polling numbers in 1961), and as many as nine and a half million of them had a favorable impression of the organization.[34] Indeed, Westin points out that at what was arguably one of the most notorious moments of the movement's history, when Welch accused President Eisenhower of being a "dedicated conscious agent of the Communist conspiracy," over three and a half million Americans still believed it was a patriotic organization.[35] These factors suggest that although it was limited in size, Welch's organization was successful in publicizing its message, and its influence extended beyond what we would today classify as the far right.

Although Webster's conspiratorial architecture made its way across the Atlantic earlier in the 20th century, it was therefore through Welch and the John Birch Society that it was most effectively disseminated. Welch not only utilized Webster's conceptualization of a worldwide conspiracy, but he also adopted her view that this conspiracy was directed by a powerful hidden force. Welch is popularly known for his dire warnings regarding Communism, but this understanding is not a complete and accurate representation of his ideas. Welch was deeply troubled by the existence of the Soviet Union and the spread of Communism, but in his view, the Communists were mere tools of a larger conspiracy. Revilo Oliver discussed the possibility of worldwide conspiracy in a 1964 article,[36] but it was Welch's adoption of this idea that saw it become common currency within the Birch Society and well-known outside the group.

In his famous 1966 lecture, "The Truth in Time," Welch argued that behind the facade that was world politics, a mysterious group of individuals, an "increasingly all-powerful hidden command," directed human existence.[37] Welch argued that these individuals were most likely direct descendants of Adam Weishaupt's Illuminati, or at the very least, a group related to the Illuminati's leadership. Because this group is so secret, its membership is a mystery; for the sake of convenience, Welch advised his readers, he will refer to this group as "the INSIDERS."[38] Welch wrote, "The extrinsic evidence is strong and convincing that by the beginning of the Twentieth Century there had evolved an inner core of conspiratorial power, able to direct and control subversive activities which were worldwide in their reach, incredibly cunning and ruthless in their nature, and brilliantly farsighted and patient in their strategy."[39] In his analysis, Welch cites both John Robison's *Proofs of a Conspiracy,* and Abbé Barruel's *Memoirs of Jacobinism.*[40] He uses the structure of Nesta Webster's conspiratorial thinking, however, as well as her explanation for socialism and its related conspiracies. In addition, he cites her *World Revolution* directly.

Following in Webster's footsteps, Welch argued that the Illuminati had first exercised their power in the "planning and precipitating [of] the holocaust known as the French Revolution"[41] and that it was in that upheaval that the conspirators developed and practiced the techniques their Communist minions used during the 20th century: undermining rulers and governments; destroying religion and supplanting it with reason; fomenting mob uprisings; using terror to silence opposition; and manufacturing smear to destroy enemies of the revolution.[42] Using these tactics, the INSIDERS had orchestrated all the major political events of the 20th century, both within the United States and in the international sphere, including the instigation of both world wars. Welch therefore warns his readers that

> today Moscow and Washington are, and for many years have been, but two hands of one body controlled by one brain. You do not have your left hand fight your right hand, or go through the motions of doing so, unless it is to amuse or deceive children, or to distract their attention from other matters while you are putting them to sleep. And these observations clearly apply to the show that is now being staged in Vietnam.[43]

For Welch, the political disorder of the age, coupled with the breadth of the conspiracy, meant that the time was at hand for his fellow citizens to rise up against the conspirators' control, "a mighty uprising of the incalculable forces of man's moral principles, love for freedom, and common sense."[44]

There was, perhaps, good reason for America's openness to conspiracy thinking in the 1960s. As noted above, international instability and the threat of nuclear weapons were an ever-present concern, and domestically, significant social and political changes were sweeping the country. The civil rights movement, anti–Vietnam War protests, feminism, Vatican II and its aftermath, and the birth control pill were just a few of the challenges to the traditional social and political landscape. These forces were not always accommodated peacefully; as Patterson writes, "[C]onfrontation, violence, and social disorder indeed seemed almost ubiquitous in America during the mid- and late 1960s."[45] His view is that the 1960s polarized the American public. Divisions that already existed were exacerbated, and fault lines that had been obscured were exposed. Traditional values were under assault on a variety of fronts and these conflicts polarized conservative and liberal Americans.

In addition, the government itself appeared to be intervening more in citizens' lives, both legitimately (in terms of the development of new public policies, including civil rights legislation and Medicare, among others) and also somewhat questionably. During its heyday, the Federal Bureau of Investigation's Counter Intelligence Program identified domestic organizations it believed were a threat to national security and saw its agents infiltrate many of these groups with a view to neutralizing them. By its own admission, many of these efforts "abridged" First Amendment rights,[46] and it investigated individuals such as Eleanor Roosevelt and groups such as the Southern Christian Leadership Conference, which it identified as a "hate group."[47] The Central Intelligence Agency also engaged in dubious activities, intervening in the affairs of particular national communities within the United States[48] and supporting behavioral control research at dozens of American universities.[49]

As the federal government expanded its responsibilities and thus lent credence to suggestions that its monitoring of and intervention in Americans' lives was exceeding reasonable limits, suspicions that it was also engaging in nefarious activities against its own citizens were building. Some of these concerns were later justified. In 1975, for example, it was revealed that the FBI had engaged in 238 illegal burglaries against "dissident groups."[50] The CIA was likewise engaged. In 1974, it came to light that the agency had spied on students at Columbia,[51] and in 1976, that it had maintained secret relationships with several hundred faculty members at other universities and colleges, eight years after President Johnson barred the organization from having relationships with scholarly institutions in the United States.[52] These activities of course represent just a small segment of its remit; during the 1960s it also used American students, domestic charitable organizations and private American research foundations in international intelligence operations.[53] Joseph Kraft remarked in his assessment of these interventions, their perpetrators, and the media's capacity to discover what occurred that "[g]iven this choking miasma of conflicting and twisted motives, there is no way ordinary citizens or even experienced reporters and congressmen can be sure about who is doing what to whom and for which purpose."[54] Notably, Kraft's foremost concern was that these many revelations would lead American citizens to become so gullible that they would believe their government was engaging in virtually anything and everything. This era of rampant government misbehavior was punctuated by Watergate, a scandal that suggested politicians were prepared to engage in activity that was clearly illegal in order to protect their power. In its wake, Kraft wrote, nothing can be excluded as "impossible."[55] With these events, a number of significant political incidents, including the 1960s assassinations of John F. Kennedy, Martin Luther King Jr., Malcolm X, and Robert F. Kennedy became the subjects of conspiratorial speculation.

In the mid-20th century, a trajectory developed that saw conspiracy theory popularized first as a response to the threat of the Soviet Union. The most public of these conspiracists was, of course, Senator Joseph McCarthy. His witch hunt generated paranoia and destroyed lives, but ultimately it collapsed. Pipes argues that this is because the senator was simply unable to substantiate his claims,[56] but as we have seen, it is also the case that conspiracy thinking does not ever have much to do with actual evidence. Anti-Communist conspiracy thinking did not, therefore, disappear. It continued with a new vanguard, and in a new form.

Robert Welch had at first been content to identify the Communists as the major villains in American politics. His reading of Nesta Webster, however, soon convinced him that the conspiracy was far more extensive than he originally thought. Webster's notion of a single evil mastermind driving a multipronged conspiracy explained how even the American president could be under its control. In this way, the fear that Communists had infiltrated the American government became the conviction that evil forces were directing that government. Political events and conspiracy theory therefore came together as they had in the early 20th century.

In addition to this, the architecture of modern conspiracy theory provided a framework for a variety of international conspiratorial ideologies in a globalizing world. Small scale and single event conspiracies might exist, but more common were concerns regarding worldwide conspiracies. Nesta Webster's identification of an evil confederacy's international conspiracy to dominate the world and her rallying cry to protect Britain from this threat was a prototype. In mid-20th-century America, the confederacy featured Socialists and Illuminati; in the late 20th century, this threat became "the New World Order."

Today, the phrase "New World Order," taken from a 1991 speech by President George H. W. Bush, is shorthand for one of the most popular formulations of modern conspiracy theory in the United States.[57] As Barkun points out, the phrase was intended to convey the importance of collective security (the idea that an attack against one nation is an attack against all, to ensure the security of all states), but to conspiracy believers, it suggests a secret cabal engaged in an attempt to control the world.[58] Removed from is context, the phrase is ominous enough to sound threatening and vague enough to suit a multiplicity of conspiracy theories, all of which suggest alien powers are taking control of the United States. Barkun outlines just a few of the theories that utilize this phrase, including:

> the systematic subversion of republican institutions by a federal government using emergency powers; the gradual subordination of the United Nations to a world government operating through the United Nations; the creation of sinister new military and paramilitary forces…the permanent stationing of foreign troops on U.S. soil; the widespread use of black helicopters to transport the tyranny's operatives; the confiscation of privately owned guns; the incarceration of so-called patriots in concentration camps run by FEMA; [and] the implantation of microchips…for surveillance and mind control.[59]

The idea of such a "New World Order" suggests a growing discomfort with the implications of international politics for the welfare of the United States.

As well as these global concerns, this new form of conspiracy thinking was also inclined to be critical of the American government, often going so far as to suggest it had become the conspiracy's dupe. This development was a departure from Nesta Webster's analysis. As will be recalled from chapter 3, Webster was critical of the British government, but for her, that institution was always a necessary part of resisting the conspiracy. Her novel, *The Secret of the Zodiac,* told the story of a conspiratorial takeover of the British government and the British Empire, but it was intended as a warning to the British people of what could happen if they were not careful. It was not a direct assessment of the political situation during her lifetime.[60] For McCarthy and the Birch Society, however, the American government was a part of the problem. As noted above, Robert Welch, for example, identified President Eisenhower as a "dedicated, conscious agent of the Communist Conspiracy."[61]

The social upheaval of the Cold War years also left its mark on the USSR. No doubt Welch would have been surprised to learn that the Communists were as worried about the Illuminati as he was. As Johnson points out, Valery Nikolaevich Emelyanov, a Soviet academic, spent much of the 1970s spreading news of a Zionist/Freemason plot to take over the world.[62] In his view, the plot also included a mixed bag of international agents, including Amnesty International, Leon Trotsky, and the Carter administration. This curious parallel suggests once again that for some individuals, conspiracy thinking fulfils an important function during periods of social change and political unrest.

Mid-20th-century conspiracy theory therefore established two of the most important tenets of conspiracy theories as we know them in the 21st century. One can say with almost absolute certainty that when we read such theories today that they will tell us that the conspiratorial perpetrators—whoever they may be—are engaged in action that is international in scope. We will also likely be told that they control our government. Concern regarding the increased economic integration of Canada, the United States, and Mexico, for example, is often framed as an assertion that a conspiracy exists for a North American Union (NAU). Daneen Peterson, an anti-NAU activist, opened his speech at a Washington rally by declaring:

> Today I will reveal to you the betrayal of the American people by a government cabal who are bent on destroying our sovereignty in order to create a North American Union. The miscreants include many who function at the highest levels in our government. Many hold membership in the Council on Foreign Relations (CFR) and the Trilateral Commission and pursue a subversive agenda. The cabal is deliberately circumventing the U.S. Congress and 'We the People' in blatant violation of our Constitution. Collectively they are committing **TREASON**.[63]

The importance of these contributions to modern conspiratorial thinking should not be underestimated. In a rapidly globalizing world, the conspiratorial inclination is to see enemies everywhere, and in an environment where national government has become extremely complex, and its bureaucracy immense, conspiratorial thinkers assume that it is evil in both its nature and its intent.

By the time Robert Welch published *The Blue Book of the John Birch Society*, he was regarded as outside the mainstream. The *New York Times Sunday Magazine* had published an article that condemned the radical right's conspiratorial view of history and its tendency to distrust democracy,[64] and the more mainstream right also sought to distance itself from the organization. William Buckley undertook a deliberate campaign to attack the John Birch Society directly, hoping to alienate its leadership from its members. He openly questioned Welch's assessment that the civil rights movement was part of the Communists' efforts to take over America, and that Medicare destroyed "the independence and integrity of American physicians."[65] As Bjerre-Poulson points out, this tactic was not particularly successful in dividing the Birch Society. Of the first 200 responses to Buckley's attack, only two supported him.[66] It did, however, initiate the process of distancing the mainstream right from Welch's and the Birch Society's conspiratorial speculations. In his analysis of this period, Edwards characterizes Robert Welch and other "conspiracy addicts," along with anti-Semites, racists, armed militants, and fundamentalist preachers as "the dark side of the Right."[67] In his view, these ideological extremists had to be effectively marginalized before the right could become politically influential. He writes of 1960s conservatism, "[A]ll of these doomsayers and paranoiacs were *in* the movement, they were not *the* movement, which as it grew and matured relegated them to the outer reaches of the Right, where most of them withered and eventually died."[68] While these groups might have declined in their immediate political importance, strictly speaking, they did not disappear, and neither did their ideas. Instead, they continued to exist at the fringe of American politics. Nesta Webster's worries about the Illuminati's plot to control the world; Robert Welch's concerns about the Illuminati, Communism, the American government, and private institutions; and a variety of other related superconspiracy theories (ranging from speculation about UFOs and a government of aliens to concerns about Cuba and the CIA) were distilled through American society and found a home at its margins.

At the beginning of this chapter, we considered how the upheaval caused by deep transformations of the international political system created the kind of uncertainty that is conducive to conspiracy thinking. Through the 1970s and 1980s, the bipolar system continued; its time, however, was limited. If, as long-cycle scholars argue, world politics is marked by a distinct and somewhat regular pattern whereby power shifts from one global leader to another in approximate 100 to 120 year long cycles, then by the late 1980s, the United States was in striking distance of the conclusion of its time as global hegemon.[69] In Modelski's view, the decline of U.S. hegemony was also to be marked by challenges to the nation-state as an institution. He notes that while the state has been a reasonable form of global organization since the mid-1600s, it is no longer clear that this will continue in a world dominated by a global economy and international corporations with budgets larger than some states' gross national product; he might well also have added terrorist organizations to his list. While the United States emerged from the Cold War as the world's major power, this transformation occurred in an environment where the very structure of the international system was changing. While many late-20th-century conspiracy theorists worry about a New World Order that destroys national sovereignty and personal autonomy, Modelski's analysis does suggest that some new way of organizing politics is necessary. For him, the institution of the state is no longer capable of managing the international system and so will eventually give way to a more effective system of global organization. He writes:

> The global political system is still dominated by the "established" system of global leadership that is now passing through the long-cycle phase of coalition-building toward the more conflictual selection phase of Macrodecision in the next generation. New conceptions of global solidarity are being forged around the issues of nuclear and environmental security but it will take time, and another cycle, for them to find their anchors in new political institutions.[70]

The very economic power that drove the United States to become the world's superpower and supports the global economy was a key factor in the initiation of this destabilization. As with each of the world's previous hegemons, it is the superpower's very strength that eventually undermines its power.

This argument is made in slightly different terms by Wallerstein, the other long-cycle scholar whose work we considered earlier. He writes, "Global liberalism which is rational and cost-effective, breeds its own demise. It makes it more difficult to retard the spread of technical expertise. Hence over time it is virtually inevitable that entrepreneurs coming along later will be able to enter the most profitable markets with the most advanced technologies and younger "plant," thus eating into the material base of the productivity edge of the hegemonic power."[71] Wallerstein's narrow definition of hegemony means that he identifies American hegemonic power as existing for only a very limited period of time: 1945–67, and that the last half of the 20th century was in fact a period of gradual decline.[72] This analysis seems perhaps more possible when one recalls the long time frame with which Wallerstein is concerned. He notes, for example, that Britain began its decline in 1873, but it was not until 1982 that Argentina openly challenged its power.[73] America, like the hegemons that preceded it, is in its turn experiencing a similarly gradual and drawn out loss of hegemony. Wallerstein comments that after the United States became the world's dominant hegemon in 1945, Americans spent 30 years learning how to assume their responsibilities in the world, and when they had learned how to do it, their hegemony "passed its peak."[74] Where Modelski is concerned with the international system's underlying structural changes, Wallerstein writes in a reflection on the tragedy of September 11, 2001, that it is important to be able to embrace political change, for it is inevitable:

> President Bush has been offering the American people certainty about their future. This is the one thing totally beyond his power to offer. The future of the United States, the future of the world, in the short run, but even more in the medium run, is absolutely uncertain. Certainty may seem desirable if one reflects on one's privileges. It seems less desirable if one thinks that the privileges are doomed to decline, even disappear. And if it were certain that the Osama bin Ladens of this world, in all camps, were to prevail, who would cherish that certainty?[75]

Change is inevitable, and as Modelski and Wallerstein write, periods of hegemonic transformation produce instability.

Long-cycle theorists' assessment that the United States was in a period of slow hegemonic decline from the 1950s onward differs from the popular narrative of international politics at the close of the 20th century. We are more familiar with declarations that "the United States won the Cold War," than with the more subtle analyses of Modelski and Wallerstein. Both of these views, however, suggested that the 1990s would be a period of tremendous economic and political instability; the long-cycle argument, however, makes clear just how significant that uncertainty was, and how deeply "the winner" of the Cold War would be marked by changing international circumstances. Modelski suggests that the development of the global economy was transforming the very framework of international politics, and in his early 1980s article, Wallerstein prophesies the decline of American manufacturing and financial sectors.[76] Against this backdrop, the major defining element of the international system changed: it evolved from a bipolar to a unipolar system, and the United States was the sole remaining superpower. This change was important from the perspective of military spending and political planning. It also had an effect on Americans' self-perception.

For most of the 20th century, Americans defined themselves in opposition to the Soviet Union, an enemy that was perceived not just as a political threat but also a moral hazard. Communism was not just an alternative system of government; it was "evil."[77] In the context of the Cold War, this dualistic way of thinking about international politics served the United States well. As Flanagan notes, dualism "emphasizes the opposition between two forces or ideas,"[78] and in politics, it is a useful mode of thinking when one has a great enemy to defeat. It effectively defines the self and the political community. It also provides a worldview with built-in certainty. One's life and one's cause are inherently meaningful, for they are part of an historic struggle between good and evil. This dualistic way of thinking about international politics marked not just presidential speeches and government policy but also informed popular culture and public sentiment. When Soviet totalitarianism decayed, however, this form of political identity effectively evaporated.

The Soviet Union's disappearance was certainly a positive political development in terms of human freedom and democracy. For the United States, however, there were therefore additional, more ambiguous issues that emerged. In a world where there was no longer a dependable enemy, how would the single remaining superpower develop its role in the world? Following that, how would its citizens conceptualize their identity and role? The world may have been a better place, but it was far less predictable. Additionally, it left a significant vacuum in public self-understanding and discourse. As it has appeared in every period of major political instability related to hegemonic change and system volatility, conspiracy theory re-emerged as a form of public discourse.

In the late 1980s and early 1990s, the shifting grounds of economics, politics, and social relations saw increasing numbers of people turn to conspiracy thinking. Interestingly, one of the first ways in which this resurgence appeared was through the exhumations of two dead politicians and a major Hollywood project reconsidering the assassination of John F. Kennedy. In the late spring of 1991, the body of Zachary Taylor, the 12th president of the United States, was exhumed in order to determine whether or not he had died by misadventure (consuming tainted cherries at a Fourth of July parade) or had instead been the victim of a (single-event) conspiracy whereby he was poisoned for his opposition to the spread of slavery.[79] Taylor had not been poisoned, and in a subsequent column for the *Washington Post* (which appeared with a title that now seems optimistic, "A Rash of Conspiracy Theories"), Charles Krauthammer decries the sudden spike in conspiracy theories of which the Taylor disinterment is only the most recent to make headlines. The conspiracies he lists includes Carter aide Gary Sick's assertion that in 1980 the Reagan presidential campaign colluded with Iran's Ayatollah Khomeini to delay the release of American hostages and claims that Watergate was in fact a conspiracy of Alexander Haig, John Dean, and Bob Woodward to remove an innocent Richard Nixon from power.[80]

Not long after Krauthammer wrote, the body of Carl Weiss, the doctor who shot Senator Huey Long, was exhumed in order to assess whether or not he suffered from some condition that may have caused him to act irrationally. This investigation was spurred in part by a variety of conspiracy theories regarding Long's assassination, including one that suggested it was actually Long's bodyguards who shot him, and Weiss was shot to cover up their guilt.[81]

The early 1990s were peppered with other conspiratorial eruptions. *High Treason, The Assassination of JFK and the Case for Conspiracy,* by Robert J. Groden and Harrison Edward Livingstone, was on the *New York Times* Best Sellers List in late 1990 and early 1991,[82] and in 1991, too, Oliver Stone released his film *JFK.* It received mixed reviews but garnered eight Academy Award nominations, and as the *New York Times* put it, "revitalized widely held conspiracy theories in the assassination of President John F. Kennedy."[83]

Krauthammer points out the bizarre paradox of these kinds of American conspiracy theories: "What is so odd about this rash of claims that various American presidential transitions were illegitimate is that America has produced the most durable and orderly system of transferring power in history. And yet ghosts keep appearing warning of murder most foul. Why is it that Americans are so ready to believe we transfer power like the Borgias, though with somewhat more guile?"[84] Krauthammer suggests that conspiracy theories are more likely when an old worldview is destroyed and a new one is needed; they are, he writes, the product of "disorienting cultural and ideological disintegration." He is puzzled by the sudden reappearance, or "rash" of these theories in the early 1990s, however, a moment when "Bush's America is quiescent to the point of coma."[85]

With the benefit of hindsight and long-cycle theory, we can now see this particular period as precisely the time when conspiracy theory should reemerge in a more widespread form. The Cold War was over and the global economy was transforming the international state system and national economies. As a result, Americans—indeed individuals everywhere—were experiencing a form of disorientation. Krauthammer's puzzlement, however, reveals another serious issue regarding the impact of conspiracy theory. Rarely, if ever, do conspiracy theories generate meaningful political action. Conspiracy believers are not inclined to engage in political activism. Why should they bother? If mysterious and all-powerful forces control politics and economics, there is little motivation to participate. Conspiracy believers have no great affection for the political system and neither do they possess political efficacy, the sense that they can make a difference in the world. These issues point to one of the most serious problems with conspiracy beliefs. The very nature of these often unreasonable beliefs encourages citizens to absent themselves from their responsibilities as citizens. They may decide against working on a political campaign; they may choose not to vote; they may simply believe what journalists tell them; or they may ignore politics completely. Perversely, these choices may lead to the very situation they most fear. A politically inactive, ill-informed, and uneducated population is more easily misled by the rhetoric of special interests that might abuse their positions of power.

The early 1990s were therefore marked by the resurgence of conspiracy theories in public discourse, a development that in and of itself was problematic for a democratic political community. At the same time, a more troubling trend had developed. The language of superconspiracies also reappeared in the political mainstream. In the preceding half century, superconspiracy theories had migrated to the edge of American politics and remained the purview of a number of extremist groups. Their appearance as a more normalized form of talking about politics was a dangerous sign.

In September of 1990 George H. W. Bush spoke to a joint session of Congress on the Persian Gulf Crisis. It was a speech filled with the hyperbole one might expect from a Cold War victor facing down a recalcitrant challenger. Among its many rhetorical flourishes was a rhetorical phrase that heartened conspiracy believers across America. As noted above, George Bush spoke of his hope for

> a new world order…freer from the threat of terror, stronger in the pursuit of justice, and more secure in the quest for peace. An era in which the nations of the world, East and West, North and South, can prosper and live in harmony. A hundred generations have searched for this elusive path to peace, while a thousand wars raged across the span of human endeavor. Today that new world is struggling to be born, a world quite different from the one we've known. A world where the rule of law supplants the rule of the jungle. A world in which nations recognize the shared responsibility for freedom and justice. A world where the strong respect the rights of the weak.[86]

Bush's challenge to fight for peace and justice in the world was interpreted by some as a sign he was secretly advocating for a Socialist revolution. Among the most influential of those to adopt this argument was television evangelist Pat Robertson.

In 1991, Marion Gordon "Pat" Robertson published *The New World Order,* a book warning Americans of a sinister Socialist plot against the United States directed by the Illuminati and European bankers; as evidence, he cited Nesta Webster.[87] In hardcover, Robertson's book sold over half a million copies, and it was a *New York Times* best seller that year.[88] The book argues that over the course of centuries conspirators have worked toward their goal of a Socialist world government, and they are on the verge of achieving their goal. The New World Order is "a precise, systematic, and rigorously planned mechanism to manage people and nations collectively by proxy and by global authority. It is a program to ensure that principles of geographical and racial "balance" are scrupulously applied."[89]

In terms of its content, the book is notable for three reasons. First, it is clear evidence of conspiracy thinking's migration to the political mainstream. As the founder of organizations such as the Christian Coalition and the Christian Broadcasting Network, and the host of television's "The 700 Club," Robertson is a highly visible spokesperson for a significant proportion of the American population, and his open adoption of this type of conspiracy theory is indicative of the degree to which this way of thinking had permeated society. As Barkun points out, Robertson "is the first modern religious and political figure of national stature to embrace a belief in an Illuminatist conspiracy."[90] A second important point is that

Robertson, like most conspiracy theorists, alters the basic conspiratorial story to suit himself and his situation. In *The New World Order,* he effectively mixes the standard Illuminati legend with his particular brand of apocalyptic religious faith. An interesting example of this is his assessment of presidents Wilson, Carter, and Bush Sr. He comments, "[I]t may well be that men of goodwill like Woodrow Wilson, Jimmy Carter and George Bush, who sincerely want a larger community of nations living at peace in our world, are in reality unknowingly and unwittingly carrying out the mission and mouthing the phrases of a tightly knit cabal whose goal is nothing less than a new order for the human race under the domination of Lucifer and his followers."[91] Nesta Webster argued that it was necessary for Britons to defeat the Illuminati and thus protect Great Britain and Christian Civilization. In Robertson's view, Americans are charged with defending America and Christian Civilization. They are actors in a grand historical narrative about an impending apocalyptic battle and the end of time.

The final aspect of Robertson's book that merits particular attention here is that his argument is marked by a seam of apparent anti-Semitism. The Anti-Defamation League questioned the book's singling out of members of the Jewish financial elite and its repeated warnings concerning "European Bankers."[92] Robertson forcefully argued against these accusations, however, and reminded the press that his book also had a strongly pro-Jewish message. Notably, however, this supportive message is rooted in his eschatology. It does not express a beneficent wish for the well-being of Jews and Israelis; instead, Robertson's religious faith informs him that Israel's existence is required for the initiation of the end of time, and the continuing presence of Jews and Israel is necessary, only so they can be destroyed in the apocalyptic battle at history's conclusion.[93] Robertson's book therefore exemplifies conspiracy thinking in the last years of the 20th century. Its appearance marks what Modelski and Wallerstein might describe as America's decline in capacity to exert hegemonic power in the international system, as well as its ascendancy as the world's sole remaining superpower.

Exhilaration at the fall of Communism was tempered by uncertainty about the future. It is incorrect to say that this lack of certainty causes people to think in conspiratorial ways. In such situations—each and every time they have occurred in the international system—a significant number of individuals who are uncomfortable with those changes have found conspiracy thinking provides an answer as to precisely "who" or "what" is behind that change. In those periods of time, conspiracy discourse moves from the political fringe to the center of political discourse.

Superconspiracies clearly delineate good and evil, and provide their believers with a picture of the universe that is ordered and therefore comprehensible. They are most centrally, however, about power, but not in the way conspiracy theorists think that they are. On the surface, conspiracy theories are narratives that argue power is held by a secret, threatening group that aims to control the world and destroy life as we know it. The villains in these accounts, however, should be the first clue that there is an underlying and unexpressed message in conspiracy theories. The Illuminati and the Freemasons advocated democracy and freedom; in modern conspiracy theories then, they are perhaps better understood as symbolic of impending changes to the way power is distributed in society.

The next chapter considers the terrorist attacks of September 11, 2001. Modelski's and Wallerstein's analyses of the rise and fall of hegemonic power tell us much about the historical context of those tragic events. Their perspective suggests perhaps why a destabilized international system results in violence, and 20th-century strategic and technical innovations suggest how that change might be expressed. The events of September 11, however, have of course come to represent so much more than just one more example of violence in the international system. They have raised questions relevant to every level of politics, local, national, and international, and touched on critical issues for political communities that range from security concerns to the rights of domestic religious minorities, and from international economic development to immigration policy.

In addition to their very real impact on every level of government and the widest reach of policy concerns, however, the 9/11 attacks are also the focus of intense conspiratorial speculation. In the world of conspiracy theorists, 9/11 was not just a terrorist attack or mass murder, but an occasion that revealed an important meaning: the purpose of the grand conspirators, the breadth of their reach, and the lengths to which they would go to achieve their aims. As will be seen, however, the most popular of those conspiracy theories identify as their villains Jews and/or Israel, the Illuminati and/or Israel, and the U.S. government. These theories tell us much more about the interests and politics of those who adopt them than they do about the actual source and meaning of the attacks.

Chapter 5

9/11

On September 11, 2001, four passenger planes were hijacked within U.S. airspace. Two of those aircraft flew directly into the World Trade Center; one crashed into the Pentagon; and the fourth went down in a Pennsylvania field. A small number of men accomplished these acts with limited flying skills and box cutters. The nature and scope of the violence they unleashed was so extreme that their impact continues to this day. It resounds in the lived experience of individual citizens, in American domestic and foreign policy, and in global political relations. Those most directly affected by the tragedy were left to negotiate an existence without family members or friends who died that day. Others, more removed, participated vicariously in the community of grief, witnessing the loss of life and destruction through the media. The American government responded to the attacks by refining its domestic security apparatus and its foreign policy goals and practice. Within weeks, the U.S. military invaded Afghanistan, and shortly thereafter, Iraq.

In the wake of this most devastating foreign attack on the United States homeland, however, it was not critical political reflection that spread like wildfire across American political discourse. Within a week of the terrorist attacks, conspiracy theories had gained a foothold in the public mind, and in the years since 9/11, those theories have become a dominant alternative explanation to "the official story." Instead of fading away over time, Fenster argues that belief in these "alternative explanations" has instead become increasingly popular.[1] A 2006 Scripps Howard/Ohio University survey revealed how widespread conspiracy beliefs regarding 9/11 have become; with a 4 percent margin of error, it found that 36 percent of Americans suspected their government had a role in the attack, or simply allowed it to happen, in order to justify its plan to go to war in the Middle East.[2] The website

911truth.org aims "[t]o expose the official lies and cover-up surrounding the events of September 11th, 2001 in a way that inspires the people to overcome denial and understand the truth; namely, that elements within the US government and covert policy apparatus must have orchestrated or participated in the execution of the attacks for these to have happened in the way that they did."[3] According to its executive director, 911Truth's website has also seen a steady increase in traffic. In 2005, it received approximately 4,000 hits per day, but that traffic tripled within a year, to over 12,000 visits per day in 2006.[4] Another source of alternative information on 9/11 is *Loose Change,* a film aimed at uncovering the real story behind the September 11 attacks. Its promoters claim the film has been viewed over 100 million times.[5] These numbers suggest that within America, widespread interest in alternative explanations for the attacks of September 11, 2001, continues.

This skepticism is not limited to the United States. It can be found in other countries as well. An international survey, conducted in 2008, interviewed citizens in 17 nations around the globe. The survey found that when they were posed the open-ended question, "Who do you think was behind the 9/11 attacks?" a significant minority in every country responded that the U.S. government was responsible.[6] Internationally, an average of 15 percent of respondents identified the U.S. government as the culprit, but across countries, the numbers varied widely. In Britain, only 5 percent stated that the U.S. government was behind the attacks, and in Jordan, 17 percent identified the U.S. government as responsible. Interestingly, the only country surveyed whose citizens were as certain as Americans (as suggested by the Scripps Howard survey) that the U.S. government was behind the 9/11 attacks was Turkey, where 36 percent indicated this was the case. In the Palestinian territories, 27 percent identified the United States as the perpetrator, and in Egypt, that number dipped to 12 percent. One might assume that in these Middle Eastern publics, there would be a significantly greater hostility to the United States. This difference might be explained in part by the fact that in these communities, Israel is more often identified as the perpetrator, but in any case, these figures are in many ways remarkable.[7]

Taken together, the Scripps Howard and World Opinion surveys suggest that Americans' suspicion of their government is both deep and widespread. Americans are much more worried about their government than are other national communities (some of whom might well fear American military and economic power). The international survey also highlights another fact: there seems to be no generally accepted explanation for the events of September 11, 2001. Across all participating countries, and accounting for populations on five continents, communities are divided in terms of who they identify as the perpetrator: Al Qaeda, the U.S. government, Israel, or "other."[8] In addition, significant numbers in every country declare they do not know who was responsible for the attacks. This suggests that there are even more people who are suspicious of the official story and might give weight to an alternative explanation. What can explain Americans' suspicion and international confusion?

This chapter suggests that as American hegemony declined through the 1990s, the resulting shifts in international relations fostered an environment wherein it was perhaps only a matter of time before terrorism from other regions came to the United States. The type of event that occurred on September 11, 2001, could perhaps have been anticipated, although not in the way conspiracy theorists argue. International politics at the turn of the millennium were ripe for such a terrorist attack. At the close of the 20th century, the gradual decline of American hegemonic power meant instability in the international system, for state capabilities were in flux. This slow redistribution of power meant that the United States was vulnerable to challenges by other international actors, and after a century that saw the rise of nonstate international actors, and the prevalence of guerilla and terrorist warfare, the events of September 11 cannot be seen as entirely anomalous. Their brutal violence may have been unanticipated, but against the background of 20th-century politics, they were sadly not that unusual.

September 11 conspiracy theories exemplify a central argument of this book: for believers, they provide security in an uncertain world, and in that function, they also provide comfort. In scope and content, however, these belief systems are troubling and ultimately problematic for the American political community. This is true in terms of the immediate health of American democracy and also in terms of the United States' developing post-hegemonic role in the international system. Conspiracy theories may reassure their believers, but as political beliefs, they are inherently polarizing. Their strict definitions of "us" and "them" foster a dualistic politics that makes national politics uncomfortable and ugly, and at the international level, this tendency is magnified. In a historical moment where the United States must support its global leadership through alliances and compromise, conspiracy theories are therefore especially problematic.

As chapter 4 suggested, many scholars of international relations argue that the last half of the 20th century was the most recent long-cycle period, and they identify the United States as its global hegemon. Wallerstein and Modelski differ on many points, but the broad outline of their analyses suggests that American hegemony, in the sense of the United States' ability to dominate all areas significant to international relations (in particular, military power as well as economic growth and innovation), began in the late 1940s and peaked in the late 1960s. Indeed, Michael Cox comments that in the immediate post–World War II period, there may have been real limits to American power, but the United States was the pivotal political player: "[I]t was impossible to imagine the restoration and maintenance of international stability...without it."[9] Subsequently, it has continued to sustain a global order that supports its interests, though in the last years of the 20th century, this became increasingly difficult, and resulted in political and economic uncertainty and upheaval.

This narrative of great power decline is of course not the only scholarly interpretation of international politics in the last decades of the 20th century. In fact, a number of authors argue the opposite. They contend that the United States' power and influence have not suffered a decline and might even be in a renewed ascendancy during the same period. Stephen Gill, for example, argues that the distinguishing factor of late-20th-century international relations was the process of globalization, whereby states in general lost effective control over economic forces. For Gill, the surging power of unchecked global capital has reshaped international relations and created a "political impasse for the old frameworks of politics."[10] It has been extraordinarily difficult for traditional political practices to exert meaningful limits on the power of the global economy. That said, however, Gill also argues that of all the world's powers, the United States is best placed to maneuver itself to utilize this situation to its own advantage. Its political leadership and economy are in part responsible for the process of globalization, and its residual abilities mean it can still dominate the system.[11]

Cox points out that other scholars fall into this category as well, including the influential Joseph Nye and Samuel Huntington (the latter most famous for his argument that the world was heading toward a "clash of civilizations").[12] Cox pithily suggests that this school of thought might well be called "the empire strikes back," but as his argument makes clear, Gill's, Nye's, and Huntington's arguments, despite their diversity, all suggest significant political upheaval was occurring during the 1990s. Gill terms these problems as "greater social polarisation and a general crisis of the state and of political authority";[13] Nye argued that a state-centric view of power was no longer sufficient, and Huntington suggested that reassertion of Western leadership is necessary.[14] In Cox's view, however, they are each in some way correct. The United States does remain the world's leading nation. These ideas suggest two interrelated tasks face the American government: adapting to a transformed international environment and reconceptualizing its understanding of power.

Whether the United States is experiencing a period of hegemonic decline or the upheaval of the last 20 years is only a small hiccup in a readjustment phase, it is evident that significant political and economic change occurred in the last two decades of the 20th century. As indicated in the previous chapter, this type of instability and uncertainty is a key factor in the development of conspiracy theories and, indeed, it was during this era that conspiracism began to play an increasing role in American public discourse.

In addition to the long-range view of hegemonic rise and fall, two other features of relations within the world system are worth mentioning in this context. Both are concerned with the nature of international conflict. The 20th century saw significant change in the practice of international armed conflict. From its origins, the modern state system provided—in the form of international law—clear limits to the ways in which states could engage in war. Western international law rests on the assumption that there is a distinction to be made between combatants and civilians; legal combatants wear uniforms or other identifiable symbols, and can engage in armed hostilities with others likewise identified. Civilians and their homes and cultural institutions are off limits in international conflict. In part because of this, traditionally war was fought on an identifiable battlefield, a fact that helped to emphasize the distinction between legal combatants and civilian noncombatants.

In the 20th century, however, these traditional distinctions broke down. From World War I through the Vietnam War, civilian casualties became a significant percentage of total casualties. As Mary Kaldor points out:

> The tendency to avoid battle and to direct most violence against civilians is evidenced by the dramatic increase in the ratio of civilian to military casualties. At the beginning of the twentieth century, 85–90 per cent of casualties in war were military. In World War II, approximately half of all war deaths were civilian. By the late 1990s, the proportions of a hundred years ago have been almost exactly reversed, so that nowadays approximately 80 per cent of all casualties in wars are civilian.[15]

Tallying the numbers of casualties during warfare is always a dubious business, for in times of conflict, it is sometimes difficult to identify with certainty who constitutes a combatant and who is a citizen, and there are, as Adam Roberts points out, many ways that civilians can become casualties; they may be injured or killed as a direct result of hostilities or they may suffer disease (mental and or physical) or sexual violence.[16] Available statistics may or may not include all of these possibilities, and it is therefore difficult to compare them effectively. It is, however, clearly the case that over the course of the 20th century, it was increasingly dangerous to be a civilian in the world's conflict zones.

Further evidence of a breakdown of the traditional distinction between combatants and civilians occurred with the use of guerilla warfare as a major tactic in late 20th-century wars. It was a means by which informal armies, not necessarily under any state's control, could engage in effective conflict with better disciplined and more technologically advanced military forces. To be successful, however, guerilla warfare depends upon the element of surprise; insofar as it is possible, combatants do not distinguish themselves from the civilian population. They flout the traditional distinction between combatants and civilians and in fact use the expectations created by that distinction as a way to gain a military advantage over their adversaries. Evidence of the increasing use of guerrilla tactics and the problems this posed for states can be found in 20th-century efforts to somehow regulate this form of conflict and its natural extension, terrorism. The 1970s Geneva Protocols I and II were one such effort. As an element of international law, however, they were, and remain controversial.[17] Those documents seemed to challenge the notion that states had a monopoly on the use of force. For national governments, granting even limited recognition to guerrilla combatants lends them a legitimacy that is problematic.

By the last decades of the 20th century, other forces were also wearing away at state sovereignty. The 1990s saw the forces of globalization accelerate and begin to alter both the political and the economic landscape in new ways. It was no longer entirely clear that any government, even if it wished to, could halt this transformation. Even the U.S. government, whose economic principles and policy played a large role in this process, was not immune. While some analysts interpreted these changes as a move toward a peaceable global village, others have argued that it instead represents "a decline of the powers of self-government, growing economic insecurity, and an attack on America's values....Meanwhile government has proved itself unable to protect Americans from these challenges, as it is rendered powerless and subservient in the face of global changes."[18] These views are, of course, extremes. It is safe to say, however, that as the world's leading economic power, the United States now functioned in a global economic environment that was in the process of deep transformation, and for which the rules were unclear.

As the 21st century dawned, therefore, the United States faced significant challenges. It remained the world's dominant power, but in economic and political disputes, it appeared less capable of consistently ensuring its desired outcome. In this environment, the traditional categories of civilian and combatant were breaking down, and in addition, the post–Cold War environment saw a general shift in states, their boundaries, and allegiances, a situation that led to further uncertainty. Notably, too, the forces of globalization were reshaping international economic relations. All of this change and uncertainty—which presented particular problems for the world's leading political and economic power—also challenged the state system itself. The free market economy wears down national sovereignty. As Robert Reich argued, all the world's nations are:

> undergoing precisely the same transformation as the United States, but all participating in essentially the same transnational trend. Barriers to cross-border flows of knowledge, money, and tangible products are crumbling; groups of people in every nation are joining global webs. In a very few years, there will be virtually no way to distinguish one national economy from another except by the exchange rate of their currencies—and even this distinction may be on the wane.[19]

Reich's assessment may have exaggerated the facts of the situation, and/or he may have been significantly ahead of his time, but all the same, the effects of globalization on national economies are undeniable, both through the 1990s and the early years of this century.

Alongside these developments, changes occurred with respect to issues of state security. Guerilla warfare and international terrorism had become an acknowledged facet of international politics. They were recognized in international law, and this recognition, somewhat ironically designed to protect civilians and support movements of national liberation, was a tacit acknowledgment that in international politics, states no longer necessarily had a monopoly on the use of force.

Technology, of course, facilitated those changes; most notably, within the past 20 years, the rise of new digital technologies has fostered economic integration as well as the development and spread of security and weapons technology. The Internet, so critical in the resurgence of conspiracism, provided a means by which information could be widely—and sometimes indiscriminately—disseminated. Internet use facilitated international communication and helped to further deepen globalization among national populations, but also provided a source of information and a means of communication for those who were not interested in integration with the established order, but instead wished to destroy it. A study by the United States Institute of Peace, for example, found that terrorists also use the Internet and do so in particular ways.[20] In some respects, their use parallels that of other individual users. First and foremost, they do so because it provides them with a wealth of information. As Donald Rumsfeld remarked of an Al Qaeda training manual found in Afghanistan, "Using public sources openly and without resorting to illegal means, it is possible to gather at least 80 percent of information about the enemy."[21] In addition, it also provides a means for them to communicate with one another.

Like other political interest groups, terrorists also use the Web to publicize their message, raise money, and attract new members. Weimann points out that in these efforts, they rarely celebrate their use of violence. Instead, they emphasize that it is their last resort, and argue that in their weakness, violence is the only way they can fight back against their vastly more powerful enemies.[22]

Most importantly, however, the existence of the Internet facilitates one of the most important aspects of modern terrorism: its network structure. Where traditional forms of organization functioned with a top-down hierarchical structure, modern technological advancements "now make it possible to think of people, as well as databases and processors, as resources on a network."[23] This is a much more flexible structure and makes networks more efficient at adapting to sudden change and evading pursuit. For these reasons, Weimann argues, "terrorists are increasingly likely to be organized in a more decentralized manner, with arrays of transnational groups linked by the Internet and communicating and coordinating horizontally rather than vertically."[24] The Internet and these organizational innovations also make terrorist groups much more difficult for states to track and destroy: dispersed and distinct cells can communicate quickly and coordinate their actions; communications costs are reduced; and the depth and volume of information network members can share is increased.[25] For terrorists, the benefits of the network structure are clear. As Barry Cooper points out, Al Qaeda's network structure allowed it to effectively attack the 20th century's major powers, the Soviet Union and the United States,[26] and more recently, Great Britain. In each of these cases, a hierarchically organized state found it difficult to anticipate and fight an attack by a horizontally organized network.

The major political trends of the 20th century provide an important context for the events of September 11, 2001. Through those 100 years, the United States rose to become the world's hegemonic power, and while it continued to be the world's leading power, by the turn of the century, it no longer seemed unassailable. It could still effectively achieve the outcomes it desired, but more often it accomplished its goals through alliances and cooperation rather than through the strength of its reputation and the exertion of raw military power. The forces of globalization were also eroding the economic power of the state. Multinational corporations and banks, although not under the control of the U.S. government, had come to symbolize the power of the ever-expanding global economy. Those outside the scope of its reach, and those who did not benefit from it, directed their energy at the state they saw as its most direct beneficiary, the United States. Against this backdrop, nonstate actors proliferated. Guerrilla warfare became the tactic of choice for populations engaged in wars of national liberation, to such an extent that it was formally recognized in traditionally state-centric international law. In regions of the globe suffering severe economic and political oppression, political figures used the language of religion to motivate their adherents to engage in terrorist acts that would cause harm to the United States and result in their own deaths. In this endeavor the Internet played a major role, providing information and facilitating communication. It created a particular kind of social network: a terrorist network.[27]

This narrative highlights the fact that the events of September 11, 2001, can be understood not as an aberration but a tragedy waiting to happen, given the condition of the international political sphere, the increasing likelihood in modern conflict that civilians will be victims, the development of the techniques of war, and the propensity of human beings to believe they know God's plan for the world and believe they are his chosen few.

Earlier chapters in this book suggest reasons why so many Americans were open to conspiracy theories in the last years of the 20th century. This chapter has further explained how profound the political change of that era was, and how destabilizing for both individuals and states. It should not therefore be surprising that in the wake of September 11, conspiracy theories emerged. Olmstead comments that most American conspiracy theories concern wartime decision making or national tragedies.[28] The events of September 11, 2001, can be understood to fall into both of these categories, and there are so many conspiratorial explanations for them and the events that followed, it would be impossible to examine them in detail here.

It is possible, however, to categorize these theories by distinguishing them on the basis of who they identify as responsible, and this categorization reveals three main groups: theories that identify Jews and/or Israel as the driving force behind the events; theories that argue some secret society, for example, the Illuminati, was responsible for the events; and finally, there are those that argue the American government and its agents were responsible for the tragedy. It should be noted that these categories are not completely distinct, nor are they entirely comprehensive. Many theories contain some combination of these villains, for example, the American government in league with the Israeli Mossad, or the Illuminati and the American government together, or even sometimes none of these, but other interested parties, for example, the owners of the World Trade Center building, anxious to avoid paying for renovations.[29]

In the first group of theories, those that argue Jews and/or Israel were behind the attacks, there are several distinct subgroups. These include the argument that the Israeli Mossad was responsible for the attacks, that another Israeli spy ring was key to the carrying out of the plan, that Israeli technology companies were involved, and finally, that the Jewish owners of the World Trade Center were to gain millions from the buildings' destruction, and thus undertook their demolition for financial reasons.[30] As support for these ideas, other claims are often made, including the notion that 4,000 Jews who worked at the World Trade Center stayed home from their jobs on September 11.[31] As Manning and Romerstein point out, not one element of this story has ever been substantiated by evidence. They track its development in the days following the terrorist attacks and make clear how even a limited knowledge of statistics makes its claim extremely unlikely:

> It appears to be based on concern expressed by the Israeli government for the fate of 4,000 Israelis resident in New York, a small number of whom worked at the World Trade Center. Within a matter of days it was no longer 4,000 Israelis, but 4,000 Jews; then reports appeared that "not a single Jew" died on September 11. It was easy to rebut as the list of victims was printed on many

reputable Web sites…about one out of every dozen names was Jewish. That matched U.S. Census Bureau data, which showed 9 percent of New York's population is Jewish.[32]

If you are inclined to be interested in this type of belief, however, it is unlikely you will be convinced by statistical inference. These types of 9/11 conspiracy theories are frequently linked to other, more expansive anti-Semitic doctrines. They assume that Jews were involved in 9/11 in part because they want to control the world.

The Anti-Defamation League argues that this type of attack on the Jewish population is not new but instead simply the latest formulation of anti-Semitism.[33] In its report on 9/11 conspiracy theories, however, the League points out one particularly problematic innovation linked to these ideas: "[T]heories about the 9/11 attacks are novel in that they have united disparate groups of Jew haters. In an unprecedented and very disturbing way, white supremacists, far-right extremists and Muslim and Arab propagandists are exchanging and echoing information, ideas and conspiracy theories regarding the attacks, particularly through the Internet. Their increased communication may lead to more cooperation between groups which have previously had very little in common except for a shared hatred of Jews."[34] Conspiracy theories that identify Jews and/or Israel as responsible for the September 11 attacks are therefore perhaps best understood as part of a longer tradition of anti-Semitic conspiracy theories. They support those who are predisposed to scapegoat that particular religious minority, and as will be discussed in the following chapter, they are dangerous. They can, and frequently are, used as a justification for violence. These theories exemplify the ways in which conspiracy theories emphasize the difference between good and evil, and how in doing so, they distinguish between "us" and "them." In this way of thinking, supposed villains and outsiders are often argued to be outside the moral community and even subhuman.

A second category of conspiracy theories is the large and diverse group that argue secret societies such as the Illuminati and Freemasons were behind September 11. These theories are the direct heirs of the ideas that emerged in 1700s Europe. In that era, they were a response to democratization and the uncertainty that it posed for the European political community. Much as modern concern regarding a supposed Jewish conspiracy is not new, the same holds true for secret-society conspiracy theories. Both forms of conspiracism are merely the most recent version of centuries-old themes. In the case of those belief systems identifying Jews and Israel as villains, that theme is scapegoating, and its most extreme expression is anti-Semitism and violence. In the case of secret societies, the most obvious motif is the quest for certainty.

The political philosopher Thomas Hobbes argued that human beings are distinct from other species in part because they are curious, and that this desire for knowledge and control of our environment is the root of many of our scientific achievements.[35] At the same time as we are driven to search for answers, however, it is also true that in many cases we cannot control our environment. International relations scholars would argue that the events leading up to September 11 were essentially unpredictable and that the attacks themselves were not preventable, no matter how careful airport security screened passengers. For many individuals, however, this is not a satisfactory answer.

As has been noted in earlier chapters, assertions that secret societies are behind the events of world history are usually attempts to obtain a more satisfactory answer and to attribute human meaning to what others see as essentially random events. With reference to September 11, for example, one author argues, "Osama bin Laden was only carrying out part of the plan which originated from the Illuminati. If American, British, and Israeli Intelligence really wanted a man out of the way, they would get him no matter how rich or powerful or protected he might be. Osama bin Laden is alive today only because the Illuminati wants him to be alive."[36] Proof of the Illuminati's involvement can be found in the prevalence of the number 11 in elements of the day's events, for example: the date of the attack (9+1+1=11; each building had 110 stories; after September 11 there are 111 days in the end of the year; the Twin Towers standing side by side looked like the number 11; the first plane to hit the towers was Flight 11; and the state of New York was the 11th state added to the Union).[37] These arguments are the best and clearest example of this mode of analysis.[38]

In times of deep structural change, the certainty these frameworks provide is appealing. It too, however, can in some situations become problematic. In its most acute expression, this type of resistance can prevent participation in the political system. As Fenster points out, while conspiracy theories are one way individuals can voice their concerns, in the end, they are not politically effective. They purport to empower believers, but in fact they serve as a replacement for real political knowledge and engagement.[39] In democracies, these tendencies are undesirable, both for the individual and the state concerned. These considerations will be considered further in the next chapter, but it is worth briefly reflecting on them here. Citizens may lose their sense of efficacy and retreat from even a limited involvement in their government, such as monitoring its activities and/or voting. Without the advice of all of its citizens, a democratic government is weakened, and without effective monitoring, it may become corrupt or engage in actions not supported by its citizens. Indirectly, it might therefore lead to the situation that the third group of conspiracy believers most fears.

Almost a decade after the events of September 11, 2001, however, it is this third category of conspiracy belief that seems to have most directly influenced mainstream American culture: the conviction that the U.S. government colluded in the events of that day, a concern that is expressed in a variety of ways. There are those who believe that the American government simply knew about the attack but did nothing to stop it, those who believe the government was involved in planning the attack but did not participate in its execution, and those who believe that the government both planned and executed this horrific attack on its own citizens. Again, surveys suggest that approximately one-third of Americans hold these types of beliefs.

Earlier chapters in this book have suggested that there are good reasons for Americans to be suspicious of their government. In her analysis of the rise of conspiracy theories in the United States, Kathryn Olmsted points out that during the 20th century, the American government grew in size and power, as well as its policy remit. She argues that the most significant change in 20th-century conspiracy thinking is the fact that American citizens have come to suspect their own government, arguing that "government officials lied to citizens, dragged the peaceable American people into foolish wars, and then spied on and oppressed the opponents of war."[40] For Olmsted, a historian, there are good reasons why Americans became so suspicious of their own government; she points out that since World War I, the American government has engaged in secret conspiracies, both against other states and against its own people (for example, the Iran-Contra Affair and experiments on African American men in the Tuskegee syphilis study), that the government has used conspiracies as explanations for its own policy decisions (for example, its use of "communist conspiracy" discourse through the Cold War years), and finally, that the government has spied on its citizens, in programs of questionable merit (for example, the FBI's COINTELPRO in the 1960s).[41]

In the case of September 11, the political leadership's attempts to mask its own incompetence, coupled with a series of decisions that cast doubt on whether or not it really wished to discover the truth, provided further evidence for those inclined to believe a conspiracy must be at work. Their beliefs are further substantiated—they believe—by their government's behavior. In the aftermath of the terrorist attacks, the U.S. government engaged in the same pattern of activities that Olmsted argues provoked this sea change in conspiracy thinking. It has conducted secret actions in order to capture Al Qaeda members, and in that effort, held individuals (both nationals and foreigners) at a secret prison in Guantanamo Bay, Cuba. In addition, it is engaged in a dubiously titled "War on Terror" (for how can one engage in a war against a tactic?) that served as justification for foreign policy decisions to engage in major international conflicts in Afghanistan and Iraq, and in which thousands of Americans have lost their lives. Finally, it has spent untold millions in further developing a national security apparatus that is directed not just at assessing foreign threat but also at its own citizens. In this effort, the most recent development is the Transportation Security Administration's use of full-body backscatter X-ray scanners for pre-flight airport security. These devices, which have been dubbed "naked scanners," provide invasive images of individual bodies that reveal genitalia and personal sanitary protection, not just whether or not an individual is concealing a weapon or explosives. As if these images were not enough, the process requires that flyers be exposed to radiation.[42] Together, these practices suggest that there may be good reason for the persistence of conspiracy theories concerning 9/11. The theories themselves may be unreasonable, but suspicion of the government and its motives might well seem warranted. Continuing speculation regarding Barack Obama's birthplace is just one example of other ways these concerns are expressed. In the general scheme of things, however, evidence suggests that vigilance with respect to government practice would be a more meaningful and worthwhile endeavor.

Human existence is fraught with uncertainty, and our achievements are limited and frequently temporary. In the grand sweep of history, states and empires rise and fall, and the world goes on. The events of September 11, 2001, emphasized the fragility of human life and the uncertainty of political existence. A fundamental difference between scholarly analyses and conspiracy theories is that the former stress uncertainty and change, but conspiratorial arguments emphasize continuity, identify specific villains with specific goals, and are marked by an absolute conviction regarding an underlying purpose for political events. In this way, they are potentially pathological. This issue is explored in the next chapter.

Chapter 6

Extremism and Apathy: The Conspiratorial Paradox

Today, the presence of conspiracy theories in public discourse may seem like a new development, but it is not. As this book has shown, at the origin of the modern state system, and in times of economic and political uncertainty through the 20th century, conspiracy theories became a feature of the way people talked about politics. Nesta Webster's transformation of the architecture of conspiracy theory helped facilitate its adaptation to the globalizing international system. Specific groups had a coordinated plan to control international and domestic political life, and their power extended secretly through a variety of forces around the world. Webster's mythology of secret societies provided an explanation for the chaos of the international economic and political environment. In the documented historical record, the Knights Templar, Freemasons, and Illuminati were harbingers of political change and that, combined with their operational secrecy, made them apt symbolic anchors for conspiratorial beliefs.

The connection of conspiracy theories with political upheaval, and particularly, their rise in popularity during times of long-cycle change, highlights the fact that at their core, conspiracy theories are theories of power. They purport to explain the location of power and how it works in the world. Analytically, however, this perspective also makes clear that they are better understood as theories of powerlessness. They hold appeal for cultures that are losing control of their political environment, and they are most appealing among those who have little or no meaningful power. In these situations, as Ray Pratt remarks, conspiracy theories "are neither silly nor irrational reaction to imagined plots, but a reasoned response to the real-life experiences of real people."[1] Among other things, conspiracy theories therefore tell us much about how at any given time, power is utilized and perceived.

It is interesting to note, for example, that the limited number of American studies on conspiracism suggest that minorities are more likely to hold conspiracy beliefs than are members of the majority population.[2] Abalakina-Paap et al. comment that this may be the result of discriminatory behavior by the majority, relating to a lack of trust, and a greater skepticism toward majority explanations.[3] In addition, revealed conspiracies, for example, Watergate, support generalized conspiracy belief. Concern among minority populations might well be the result of government programs targeted at their community, such as the FBI's COINTELPRO investigations and the Public Health Service's study at Tuskegee, which examined the effects of untreated syphilis on 399 African American men by withholding their treatment for the disease for 40 years.[4] Anita Waters's study of conspiracy beliefs among African Americans sheds light on why and how conspiracy beliefs can function in that population. Waters's data shows that among those she surveyed, conspiracy believers were in fact better educated than those who did not believe and more likely to have experienced both inter-ethnic cooperation and conflict than those who were skeptical of conspiracy beliefs. In addition, they were also politically active and knowledgeable about the problems their community faced.[5] In Waters's view, the explanation for these findings is complex but perhaps suggests that educated middle-class African Americans are more likely to encounter racism because their interactions with European Americans are more frequent, and likewise as their socioeconomic fortunes rise, they are more likely to question continuing general disparities between African Americans and European Americans.[6] Supporting this conclusion, Waters also found that conspiracy believers were less likely to believe that African American politicians would make a difference to race relations.[7] Waters's study was conducted in 1991; it would be interesting to see if these results would change were the study replicated following President Obama's election.

The findings in Waters's study at first seem to contradict many of the generally held assumptions about conspiracy believers. Those surveyed in her research are more engaged in politics and better educated than those who are skeptical of conspiratorial explanations. The study does, however, suggest that conspiracy believers' social, economic, and political competence allows them to identify enduring disparities between European and African Americans that have no easy explanation, and as noted above, makes it more likely that they will encounter racism. In this situation, while other reasons for this situation may be more likely, those who have exerted their own power and achieved success may find the idea of conspiracy a compelling explanation. This interpretation supports the argument that conspiracy theories are fostered by disparities in political power. In this view conspiracy theory is a form of activism, "a way of attributing blame for the complexities that led to a minority group being or feeling repressed or marginalized, and of linking the personal and the political into a single 'transcoding metaphor.'"[8]

If conspiracy beliefs are for some populations a reasoned response to their political situation, are they just another way of understanding politics, albeit an understanding that has only a minimal connection to reality? It seems clear from the patterns of their emergence and development that conspiracy theories cannot be written off as simply pathological delusions. They feature more strongly in public discourse during periods of political upheaval, and this suggests that some kind of relationship exists between the condition of the political world and conspiratorial thinking. In addition, conspiracism is substantively concerned with power, who holds it, and how it is exercised. For this reason, the appearance of conspiracy theories is of some political significance (though not the type its believers would have us believe) and provides some insight into the political condition of our age.

Conspiracism and Political Life

If event and superconspiracy theories are not just an eccentric way of explaining "why bad things happen to good people,"[9] it becomes important to consider their impact on our political communities. In fact, one does not have to look far before it becomes evident that conspiracy theory often plays a role in extremist political ideologies. The very architecture of conspiracy belief fosters antidemocratic political extremism.

Most clearly, conspiracy theories are effective at identifying who constitutes "us" and who constitutes "them." They cleanly divide the world into good and evil, categorizing humanity according to its place in the conspiratorial framework: those who agree with them are the righteous and those who do not agree with them are a part of the conspiracy, or dupes who facilitate the conspiracy's operation, and both morally and practically wrong. The use of moral language is notable here. In all such constructs, but particularly in the case of modern superconspiracy theories, believers understand their ideas to be an accurate assessment of human history, and their conspiracy theory identifies a serious threat to their particular culture, race, or nation. Indeed, Hofstadter remarked upon how for these reasons conspiracy theorists understand themselves to be real patriots, and even in the most awful actions, to be morally upstanding.[10]

While both forms of conspiracy thinking impart moral definitions to the political world, it is in superconspiracy theories that this tendency is most pronounced. Their argument that the world can essentially be divided into conspirators and victims purports to explain the entire realm of human political experience. As a result, the conspiracy theory itself becomes the believer's moral compass. On first consideration, this may not seem problematic, but the dualistic structure of conspiracy theories means that they are easily compatible with extremist political ideologies. The emphasis on "us" versus "them" in the conspiratorial framework fosters a toxic understanding of those outside one's community of believers. In his study of the psychology of fundamentalism and terrorism, Robert Young writes that such dualistic thinking causes believers to "lose the ability to imagine the inner world and humanity of others."[11] While his study is focused on a particular type of extremist religion, the comparison here is appropriate. Millenarian religious faiths and conspiracy theories have a similar structure. As Charles Strozier and Katharine Boyd argue, this is because in both such ways of thinking, human existence is understood as torn by the struggle between good and evil, and believers also share a faith that the conflict between these forces will eventually be resolved.[12] Dualistic belief systems "seek to collapse the manifold variations of a plural world into two great categories, and then urge the victory of one and the annihilation of the other."[13] The forces of right must triumph over the conspiracy. Believers assume their idea of the best political life is the one that will—and must—dominate the post-conspiratorial world.

Conspiratorialists are therefore not just fighting against the conspiracy, but they are fighting for a particular vision of the world that they believe is threatened. As the case of Timothy McVeigh illustrates, together these tendencies can become dangerous for the political community. McVeigh viewed his actions as in some way an act of national loyalty. He bombed the

Alfred P. Murrah Building in Oklahoma City as a means to attack the federal government, which in his view, had been taken over by the amorphous New World Order. He had come to believe that the American government was destroying Americans' liberty. The bombing itself is today the subject of many conspiracy theories including arguments that the Illuminati were involved,[14] as well as theories that suggest McVeigh was the victim of a larger conspiracy.[15] McVeigh himself, however, was extremely unhappy at suggestions that he was the dupe of a larger conspiratorial plan. Jon Ronson writes that while he was on death row, McVeigh was adamant that the bombing was his own work and proud of it. He felt conspiracy theories were "tainting his impending martyrdom" with their suggestions that he was not wholly responsible for the destruction.[16] Moved by his own conspiratorial understanding of American politics, McVeigh attacked the federal building, attempting to impose his views on the world. One hundred and sixty-eight men, women, and children died.

The strict moral dualism of conspiracy theories is therefore a potent political force. It is compelling in its simplicity, drawing believers who are anxious to find meaning in the uncertainty of human existence. In practice, however, it is dangerous. It provides for some a motivation to engage in violent attempts to remake the world. These outbursts are thankfully reasonably rare, but the impact of this way of thinking is also problematic in less immediately horrific ways.

The dualistic nature of conspiracy thinking may not always lead to violence, but it may still cause significant harm to the political community. In branding particular groups as outsiders, it can also foster stereotypes and social ostracism, developments that harm the health of a democracy, and which in turn also might eventually lead to violence. The clearest example of this tendency can be found in the connection of conspiracy theory and anti-Semitism.

In some event conspiracy theories, but more seriously in many superconspiracy theories, Jews are identified as shadowy puppet masters directing the world's economic and political systems, or sharing that responsibility with the Illuminati and/or Freemasons. In his examination of the history of anti-Semitism, Walter Laqueur argues that even more than racialist anti-Semitism, this notion of a Jewish world conspiracy is critical to many modern anti-Semitic doctrines.[17] Laqueur points out that the idea of Jewish conspiracy goes back to the Middle Ages, although its lineage is clearest after the French Revolution. His analysis, however, puzzles over how such a major political event could be blamed on such a powerless group.[18] As we have seen, however, conspiratorial villains do not necessarily reflect reality. Instead, they are often better understood as symbolic of changes that threaten the mainstream status quo. The Knights Templar, Freemasons, and the Illuminati were groups whose distinguishing feature was the way in which they challenged traditional modes of political power. The Jewish communities of Europe were likewise liminal groups. They were a part of society, and simultaneously apart from it, their separateness emphasized by Jews themselves, and by the larger political entities in which they lived. Governments reinforced the community's otherness by denying rights and freedoms to its members, but at the same time, the community acquired economic power. These complex and often contradictory relationships, coupled with the closed nature of the religious community, helped to make the Jews reasonable conspiratorial villains.

In addition, their success fostered antipathy. As Lindemann writes of the middle 19th century:

> Resentments focused on Jews for a number of reasons. They were prominent in the stock market in most countries, and Jewish names were linked to many of the financial scandals of the day. But the disproportionate number of Jews involved in publicly exposed wrongdoing was probably not the main issue; rather it was that Jews were now believed to be in positions of growing and decisive importance in the modern nation states of Europe. Exaggerations of that importance naturally connected to long-standing fantasies about Jews and money.[19]

In both practical and symbolic terms, the Jewish community therefore became a further center of conspiratorial fears. Unlike the Knights, Freemasons, and Illuminati, however, the Jews were in fact a real minority population whose political rights were often challenged in the European communities in which they lived. Perversely, their existence at society's margins made them the subject of conspiracy theories, and conspiracy theories positing that they possessed vast powers to control the world's economic and political life fostered anti-Semitism that helped to keep them at the social margins of European public life. Adding fuel to the fire was the Christian narrative regarding the death of Jesus. As much as the Freemasons and the Illuminati embodied the specter of secular enlightenment thinking, the idea of a Jewish conspiracy included—sometimes explicitly and some-times implicitly—some notion of the belief that "the Jews" were behind the execution of the Christian messiah. As Nesta Webster commented, "The deification of humanity by the Freemasons of the Grand Orient finds its counterpart in the deification of Israel by the modern Jew."[20]

Webster argues that a Jewish hope for world-domination is not fabri-cated by "'anti-Semites'" [quotation marks hers], but is instead a critical part of their religious tradition, which is built on a hatred for Christianity that is both cultural and doctrinal.[21] She comments that "hatred of the person and teaching of Christ did not end at Golgotha, but was kept alive by the Rabbis and perpetuated in the Talmud and the Toledot Yeshu."[22] Webster's assessment of the Jewish community is therefore both religious and political, a point emphasized by her assessment of the *Protocols of the Elders of Zion*. Although Webster was always at pains to declare that she treated the question of the Protocols as "an entirely open question,"[23] it is also the case that she reprinted the Protocols and in that way dis-seminated them,[24] and her comments are of such an indirect nature that they appear suspicious. In *World Revolution*, for example, she writes, "The truth is, then, that the Protocols have never been refuted, and the futility of the so-called refutations, as also the fact of their temporary suppres-sion, have done more to convince the public of their authenticity than all the anti-Semite writings on the subject put together."[25] Webster's analysis therefore illustrates how the conspiratorial construction of evil and one's enemies can easily become the foundation for an ideology that is poten-tially racist.

In this way, the dualistic nature of conspiracy theories functions to threaten minority populations. They are not just a political danger but also a moral threat. The Jewish community is often a target of this type of con-spiracism, and authors such as Pipes make anti-Semitism a major theme in their analysis of conspiracy theories,[26] but the architecture of conspiratorial beliefs suggests that virtually any minority group could become a victim. A quick perusal of *The Turner Diaries*, for example, illustrates this point. In that novel, the author, Andrew McDonald (a pseudonym for William Pierce), treats every minority as subhuman; no one is spared. The central character in the novel is Earl Turner, a member of "the Organization," a group of white Americans engaged in a guerilla war with "the System," Mc-Donald's name for the Jewish conspiracy that has taken over the American government.

McDonald treats other races as means rather than ends, and all non-whites are targets for the Organization, especially African Americans. He writes in one episode:

> Our people inside the military in other parts of the country had been in-structed to carry out actions…[that] involved some sabotage, arson, and demolition, but to a much greater extent it involved selective shootings. In units with a high quota of non-Whites, our people shot down Blacks at ran-dom, shouting slogans such as "White power!," with the deliberate intention of provoking a Black reaction. This was followed up by the same tactic which we used here so successfully: seizing radio stations and broadcasting spurious calls for Blacks to turn their guns against their White officers.[27]

While McDonald clearly identifies Jews as the conspiratorial masterminds, no nonwhite escapes his wrath. In this book, the line is between whites who agree with his view of the world and those of other races, and whites who disagree with him.

The Turner Diaries therefore indicates the ways in which conspiracy thinking might lead to violence; as noted above, Timothy McVeigh was inspired by its account to begin his war with the American government with the Oklahoma City bombing.[28] It is important to note, however, that the connection between conspiracy theory and violence is not necessarily a causal relationship. While in the case of McVeigh and his colleagues *The Turner Diaries* helpfully provided both conspiratorial arguments and prac-tical instructions for making a large bomb, in many cases, however, the link between idea and action is more tenuous. At the root of this issue is the fact that conspiracy theory requires of its believers that they understand outsid-ers to be of lesser moral standing. They are obstacles that must be overcome or destroyed.

A second and less immediately pathological way that superconspiracy belief can have an impact on politics is through its influence on certain communities' religious expectations concerning the end of the world. Many religious and secular groups are marked by millenarianism, the be-lief that the world is torn by an escalating conflict between good and evil, the conviction that soon that conflict will culminate in the victory of the forces of good, and the anticipation of an imminent, this-worldly salvation that will bring about the final stage of history.[29] These apocalyptic beliefs are interesting in and of themselves, but they are particularly notable for us because of their structural similarity to conspiracy beliefs. Both ways of thinking understand the world to be marked by an ongoing and escalating battle between good and evil, and both anticipate the imminent culmination of that battle, and following its resolution, the institution of a more perfect existence. As Flanagan writes, "All dualistic visions...seek to collapse the manifold variations of a plural world into two great categories, and then urge victory of one and the annihilation of the other."[30]

This structural similarity is noteworthy because it facilitates appending conspiracy theories onto the millenarian belief structure. Fenster notes this connection, and points out that this link is fairly widespread, at least in the American context: "Popular eschatology is based on a specific master narrative, it is followed through the active interpretation of events by both prophecy "experts" and many everyday fundamentalists, it is based on a mechanistic theory of power, and it shapes the political beliefs and activities of those who come to believe in it."[31] In his analysis, Fenster examines the widespread nature of eschatological religious doctrines in the United States, assessing the ways in which some of the more influential of Christian millenarians have adopted conspiracy theory. Included in his discussion are Pat Robertson, who adopted Nesta Webster's ideas, thereby facilitating the spread not just of her conspiracy theories but also her anti-Semitism, and Jack Van Impe, whose television ministry facilitated linking millennial beliefs and conspiracy theory.[32] An advertisement for one of his video sermons, for example, declares: "The Illuminati, The Trilateral Commission, The Council on Foreign Relations, the Bilderburgers, the New Agers, They have all plotted, promoted, and propagated an irreligious monstrosity designed to control the earth's six billion citizens by means of computerized technology....Discover how this one world government could be operational within mere months, how it was predicted in Bible prophecy, and what you can do to protect yourself."[33]

These types of connections can be found in a wide variety of Protestant millenarian movements in the United States. Christian Exodus, for example, is a millenarian group that intends to move thousands of its members to South Carolina and hopes to elect Christian Constitutionalists who share their conservative religious beliefs. Their membership can then dominate the state's government and enact policy that reflects their faith.[34] In addition to their religious principles, however, Exodus's members are also inclined to express conspiratorial concerns. In the words of their founder, Cory Burnell:

> The Bible tells us that the "anti-Christ," fittingly a politician, will rise to power during the creation or early existence of a world government. A 7-year period called the Tribulation will ensue....Christ will return at the end of those 7 years, destroying those in power and establishing his own kingdom of this earth....The warning signs for the end of time are increased centralization of power in ever larger governmental bodies, and the use of "false flags," terrorist attacks, natural catastrophes and financial crises as the excuse for necessity of this centralized power. It's fascinating to watch this unfold before us with the North American Union, and the collapse of the dollar.[35]

Christian Exodus's membership might be small, but its ideology is illustrative of the openness of millennial religious doctrines to conspiracy thinking. Millennial beliefs provide an explanation for why evil is at work in the world, and conspiracism explains how that evil functions.

While Exodus does not advocate violence to achieve its goals, its leadership does suggest that the membership would defend their rights if the government should challenge them:

> [W]e see the need for Christians to be secure in a sovereign state that will not participate in the North American Union, that will not allow foreign soldiers to police its streets, that will not participate in inflationary monetary policy, that will not join a world governmental system, that will protect families from having their children confiscated by foreign police because they're home schooled or taught Christianity or spanked, that will protect our right to self-defence.[36]

While Exodus has not engaged in violence, as its leader expresses here, any capacity that this group might have for violence is linked to its conspiratorial fears regarding the North American Union. Conspiracy theory can therefore have a profound influence on millenarian groups; it identifies where and how evil is at work, and in so doing, provides targets for those who wish to initiate what they view as the ultimate conflict between good and evil. In these cases, religious beliefs provide a justification for violence.

In his analysis of millennialism and conspiracy theory in American life, Barkun points out that on the basis of beliefs alone, it is extremely difficult to predict whether or not a group will engage in violence. He points out, however, that evidence suggests that one key predictor of millennial group violence is whether or not the individuals in that group feel as if they are trapped or under attack.[37] Barkun's argument is supported by two well-known examples. Aum Shinrikyō, the Japanese group that in 1995 attacked a Tokyo subway station, and Jim Jones's Peoples Temple, whose members took their lives in Jonestown, Guyana, in November of 1978, are both in this category. Each of these groups felt that they were under attack. Notably, too, both groups held conspiratorial beliefs.[38] Immediately before the Tokyo bombing, for example, Aum Shinrikyō's leader, Shōkō Asahara, prophesied that its members were "the focus of pernicious attacks by American and Japanese government forces using poison gases, and the target of a world-wide conspiracy of Jews and Freemasons."[39] Likewise, Rebecca Moore points out that members of the Peoples Temple were also informed in *Peoples Forum* (the organization's newsletter) that a conspiracy existed against them.[40]

Catherine Wessinger also concludes that it is always difficult to assess a millenarian group's potential for violence,[41] and the same holds true for conspiracy believers. In significant cases, however, the dualistic nature of conspiracy theory belief has fostered both an increased sense of persecution and a demonization of those whom they perceive to be the enemy. These factors seem to be one way in which millenarian religious hopes are channeled into violent activities.

Conspiracy belief relies on dualistic categories that can foster racism and stereotyping. In particular circumstances, it can also play a role in channeling these ideas in such a way as to justify violence. Many conspiracy believers would likely find these connections surprising, but they emerge from the very structure of conspiratorial belief systems. The cases of Aum Shinrikyō and the Peoples Temple share another ideological element. Members of both groups believed that their respective governments were involved in the conspiracy against them. In both of these situations, the group's response was extreme. The belief that one's government is actively working against individual well-being and betraying national ideals are, however, critical in the development of the diametrically opposed response to conspiracy belief: apathy and retreat from meaningful public life.

A central argument of this book is that the choice to believe in conspiracy theories can be understood as rational; in specific circumstances, and for specific types of populations, these beliefs appear to provide reasonable explanations. It is a mistake to write them off as ridiculous fantasies, for they can provide us with insight into our community's political condition. The choice of conspiratorial villains illustrates this point; the Freemasons, Illuminati, and Knights Templar are symbolic of the ways in which profound political change is seen—by some—as a threat.

It is therefore hardly surprising that the events of September 11, 2001, are the center of so many conspiracy theories. The deep-rooted change in the international political system erupted in violence so spectacular in its execution and tragic in its result that it profoundly challenged Americans' understanding of their government and its role in the world. Scholarly analyses of the international system would suggest to us that as a hegemon loses its capacity to manage international politics and economics, significant upheaval might well be anticipated. For most of us, however, the fact that such things could occur at all was a horrific shock. Over 50 years of hegemonic power lulled us into a confidence that American citizens were safe from the violence of the international system. As political analysts from the time of Thucydides onward have shown, however, relationships among states and other international actors evolve over time. In this, as in all things, the capacity for human beings to control the political world is limited. Eventually, even the world's great powers must confront this inevitability.

Following September 11, individuals' shock and dismay was experienced in the context of the development of conspiracy theory through the 20th century. Nesta Webster's conceptualization of a world in which an evil cabal expresses its will through secret societies such as the Illuminati and Freemasons is to some a compelling explanation when one is trying to understand an enemy that seems to be both everywhere and nowhere. In the view of conspiracists, the American military's difficulty finding the attacks' mastermind, Osama bin Laden, is further evidence that unseen forces were responsible. It is much more difficult to understand why and how even the world's preeminent political and military power took so long to satisfactorily conclude this operation. Indeed, many conspiracy thinkers tell us, it must be that the government knew about this attack and did nothing. The 9/11 Truth Movement details a wide range of government incompetency in its list of reasons to doubt "the official story."[42] Would a government turn on its people in this way? Sometimes incompetency is just incompetency. Again, conspiracy theories are theories about power. Conspiracy theories that blame the American government assume it has the capacity to control its political environment. Such assumptions are always mistaken, even for the world's mightiest countries.

If forces beyond your control, and even beyond the control of your government, are directing the significant economic and political events of our time, then a retreat from the political sphere is also a reasonable response. In addition to violence, therefore, conspiracy theories can also foster apathy and alienation. Conspiratorial beliefs suggest to believers that all political activity, from grassroots activism to voting, has no purpose. In political science terms, such individuals lack internal political efficacy, the sense of being able to act effectively in the political realm,[43] and external efficacy, the sense that government responds to their needs.[44] In this worldview, individual political activity is pointless, for any such engagement can have no meaningful outcome. The resulting disengagement with the public sphere is not easily overcome. Those who withdraw from political life are likely to be hostile to the political process, government, and its institutions.[45] This hostility reinforces a lack of trust, which in turn, reinforces alienation from the political system, a cycle that provides both inspiration and evidence for conspiracy beliefs.

It is interesting to note that in their distrust of government, conspiracy believers are not alone. Gallup's annual governance survey of Americans reveals a troubling picture. While trust in government was high in the 1960s, it dipped severely following Watergate in 1973, when only 40 percent of those surveyed said that they had a great deal or fair amount of trust in their president.[46] While that number gradually increased in the following 30 years to a high of 72 percent, it began a rapid and precipitous decline in 2003. By the time of the 2010 survey, that number had tumbled to 49 percent.[47] Noteworthy, too, is that distrust has spread beyond its focus on the executive branch. The 2008 survey was the first in which the percentage of those who stated they had a great deal of trust in Congress sank below 50 percent.[48] By the 2010 survey, that number had plummeted to a record low of 36 percent.[49]

Without more specific survey data, it is impossible to make any sort of causal link between conspiracy belief and this general decline in Americans' trust in their government. It is, however, certainly possible that these two factors are related. Whether or not a relationship exists between them, the concurrent rise of conspiracy belief and a general trend of declining trust in government and its institutions paint a disquieting picture for the political community's immediate future. In the long term, political apathy and/or alienation and a general mistrust of the political system are perhaps more problematic than even sporadic outbursts of extreme violence.

The health of a democratic republic requires the informed participation of its citizens; when large segments of a population choose not to participate in civic life—for any reason—a significant blow is dealt to what one might call the spiritual health of the community. Those who do not participate are harmed because their voices are not heard in government and because they do not have the opportunity to express themselves in the public realm. Classical political philosophers argued this was essential to fostering political virtue in a republican citizenry. The government is also less able to govern effectively because it does not have the guidance of the full range of its citizenry.

In this context, conspiracy theory's analysis of power is especially problematic. At the heart of every superconspiracy theory is the argument that political power is exercised by a group of evil doers who control our political, economic, and social institutions. They act in their own interest and against the public good. It is the case, however, that the political implications of conspiracy belief include the possibility that just such a situation might emerge. As John Curran remarked in 1790, "The condition upon which God hath given liberty to man is eternal vigilance; which condition if he break, servitude is at once the consequence of his crime and the punishment of his guilt."[50] In withdrawing from the political sphere, or in engaging in violence instead of reasoned debate, conspiracists risk the emergence of the very political power that they fear.

At the same time, a public sphere filled with conspiratorial discourse is also unhealthy. This book highlights the fact that although it is some cases a rational response to political crises, conspiratorial thinking is also problematic, particularly in its dualistic view of the world. As Flanagan points out, all forms of dualism, including conspiracy thinking, millenarianism, and populist political ideologies directly repudiate the pluralism of the world, upon which democracy and republicanism are based.[51] Viewed in these terms, conspiracy theory involves what political philosopher Eric Voegelin termed a "second reality."[52] It is an effort to resolve the fundamental difficulties of human existence through the creation of an ideological system that provides absolute answers, rather than facing a very complex political reality. Human life is both difficult and uncertain, and it will always be marked by disagreement and conflict. "There is," as Flanagan tells us, "no permanent end to the political process."[53] This is particularly true of the moment at which we now stand.

The process of hegemonic change suggests that the United States cannot continue to direct the world through sheer exertion of political, military, and cultural power. The prevalence of conspiracy theory in our era, however, is a response to political change that reflects that desire for domination. In response to the events of September 11, 2001, Immanuel Wallerstein wrote, "Can [we] learn to be a land that treats everyone everywhere as equals? And can we deal as equal to equal in the world-system if we do not deal as equal to equal within our own frontiers?"[54] His question recalls the fundamental founding principles of the United States and the promise they still hold. To cling to the world as conspiracy theorists see it is to hold on to a calcified understanding of power that denies the possibilities that human existence offers us. Rethinking power—and even considering a more democratized political world—reminds us of the uncertainty of existence. It may be frightening, but it may also provide us with a better world.

Notes

Introduction

1. Richard Hole, "True Conspiracies, the Illuminati, and One World Government, A Conspiracy by the International Bankers, Jesuits, Illuminati and Other Groups," http://www.trueconspiracies.com/.

2. See, for example, "Football Story," http://tribes.tribe.net/oldeschoolfootball/thread/ac4ee7da-69b7–49ce-a984–2afe5d0bc585.

3. See, for example, "Paul McCartney Really Is Dead," http://www.paulreallyisdead.com/.

4. Donald Ardell, "Don't Buy Bottled Water," May 12, 2003, http://www.seekwellness.com/wellness/reports/2003–05–12.htm.

5. The margin of error for the poll was plus or minus 3 points. Shannon Travis, "CNN Poll: Quarter Doubt Obama Was Born in US," August 4, 2010, http://politicalticker.blogs.cnn.com/2010/08/04/cnn-poll-quarter-doubt-president-was-born-in-u-s/.

6. See, for example, "David Icke You Are a Moron," http://www.abovetopsecret.com/forum/thread269247/pg1.

7. "The Glen Beck Conspiracy Theory Generator," http://politicalhumor.about.com/library/bl-glenn-beck-conspiracy.htm.

8. Ibid.

9. "Clinton: Vast Right-Wing Conspiracy is Back," Associated Press, March 13, 2007, http://www.msnbc.msn.com/id/17593375/.

10. Kyle Drennen, "CBS: Alec Baldwin 'Easy Target' for 'Conservative Junkyard Dog' Sean Hannity," *NewsBusters, Exposing and Combating Liberal Media Bias,* March 12, 2008, http://newsbusters.org/blogs/kyle-drennen/2008/05/12/cbs-alec-baldwin-easy-target-conservative-junkyard-dog-sean-hannity.

Chapter 1 I Want to Believe

1. The Global Language Monitor, "How 9/11 Changed the Way Americans Speak," September 10, 2008, http://www.languagemonitor.com/?s=9%2F11.

2. Thomas Hargrove, "Third of Americans Suspect 9–11 Government Conspiracy," Scripps News, August 1, 2006, http://www.scrippsnews.com/911poll.

3. Paul Joseph Watson, "Martin Sheen Questions Official 9/11 Story," October 29, 2007, http://www.prisonplanet.com/articles/october2007/291007_sheen_questions.htm. Lists of those who question the official 9/11 can be found at http://www.patriotsquestion911.com/media.html.

4. Jonathan Kay, "Black Helicopters over Nashville," *Newsweek,* February 9, 2010, http://www.newsweek.com/2010/02/08/black-helicopters-over-nashville.html.

5. See, for example, "American Concentration Camps," http://www.apfn.org/apfn/camps.htm.

6. *Oxford English Dictionary Online,* http://dictionary.oed.com/cgi/entry/50048058?single=1&query_type=word&queryword=conspire&first=1&max_to_show=10.

7. *Oxford English Dictionary Online,* http://dictionary.oed.com/cgi/entry/50048047?query_type=word&queryword=conspire&first=1&max_to_show=10&single=1&sort_type=alpha.

8. See, for example, James McConnachie and Robin Tudge, "Marilyn Monroe," *The Rough Guide to Conspiracy Theories* (London: Penguin Books, 2005), 17–20 and Joel Levy, "Candle in the Wind," *The Little Book of Conspiracies* (London: Key Porter Books, 2006), 92–93.

9. "Secret Kennedy Extraterrestrial Briefing Strengthens UFO Assassination Theories," *We Must Know,* June 29, 2010, http://wemustknow.net/2010/06/secret-kennedy-extraterrestrial-briefing-strengthens-ufo-assassination-theories/. See also, "Kennedy Brothers, Marilyn Monroe, and the UFO Connection: New Evidence Surfaces," June 28, 2010, and "JFK Told Marylyn [*sic*] about Roswell," Video, available at: http://www.youtube.com/watch?v=fdC2bndiwuY&NR=1&feature=fvwp.

10. Michael Barkun, *A Culture of Conspiracy, Apocalyptic Visions in Contemporary America* (Berkeley: University of California Press, 2003), 3–4. See also, George Johnson, *Architects of Fear, Conspiracy Theories and Paranoia in American Politics* (Los Angeles: Jeremy Tarcher, 1983).

11. James McConnachie and Robin Tudge, *The Rough Guide to Conspiracy Theories,* 361–69.

12. Dieter Groh, "The Temptation of Conspiracy Theory, or: Why Do Bad Things Happen to Good People? Part I: Preliminary Draft of a Theory of Conspiracy Theories," in Carl Graumann and Serge Moscovici, eds., *Changing Conceptions of Conspiracy* (New York: Springer-Verlag, 1987), 3.

13. Mohamed Al-Fayed, "Diana and Dodi, The Verdict—a Statement by Mohamed Al-Fayed," http://www.alfayed.com/dodi-and-diana/the-inquests/verdict.aspx.

14. James McConnachie and Robin Tudge, *The Rough Guide to Conspiracy Theories,* 61.

15. Brian Desborough, "Did British Intelligence Orchestrate Diana's Death?" http://www.dianaprincessofwales.net/didbritisintelligenceorchestrateprincessdi anasdeath.htm

16. Michael Barkun, *A Culture of Conspiracy, Apocalyptic Visions in Contemporary America*, 37.

17. Ted Goertzel, "Belief in Conspiracy Theories," *Political Psychology*, Vol. 15, No. 4 (1994), 735.

18. Ibid., 739.

19. Marina Abalakina-Paap et al., "Beliefs in Conspiracies," *Political Psychology*, Vol. 20, No. 3 (Sept. 1999), 642.

20. Ibid., 641.

21. Viren Swami, Tomas Chamorro-Premuzic, and Adrian Furnham, "Unanswered Questions: A Preliminary Investigation of Personality and Individual Difference Predictors of 9/11 Conspiracist Beliefs," *Applied Cognitive Psychology* (May 2009) (DOI: 10.1002/acp.1583), http://www3.interscience.wiley.com/journal/122386128/abstract.

22. Ibid.

23. Michael Barkun, *A Culture of Conspiracy, Apocalyptic Visions in Contemporary America*, 37.

24. Jeffrey Kaplan, "The Politics of Rage, Militias and the Future of the Far Right," *The Christian Century*, June 19–26, 1996, 657–62, http://www.religion-online.org/showarticle.asp?title=226.

25. Albert S. Lindemann, *Anti-Semitism before the Holocaust* (Harlow, England: Longman, 2000), 83–84.

26. Walter Laqueur, *The Changing Face of Anti-Semitism, From Ancient Times to the Present Day* (Oxford: Oxford University Press, 2006), 96–100.

27. "Satellite Network Recycles The Protocols of the Elders of Zion," The Anti-Defamation League, January 9, 2004, http://www.adl.org/special_reports/protocols/protocols_recycled.asp.

28. Michael Barkun, *A Culture of Conspiracy, Apocalyptic Visions in Contemporary America*, 38.

29. George Johnson, *Architects of Fear, Conspiracy Theories and Paranoia in American Politics*, 13.

30. Michael Barkun, *A Culture of Conspiracy, Apocalyptic Visions in Contemporary America*, 7.

31. Matthew Gray, "Explaining Conspiracy Theories in Modern Arab Middle Eastern Political Discourse: Some Problems and Limitations of the Literature," *Critique: Critical Middle Eastern Studies*, Vol. 17, No. 2 (Summer 2008), 159.

32. Michael Barkun, *A Culture of Conspiracy, Apocalyptic Visions in Contemporary America*, 3–4.

33. George Johnson, *Architects of Fear, Conspiracy Theories and Paranoia in American Politics*, 104–6.

34. Marie Gunther, "Huge Alaska Oil Reserves Go Unused," *The Spotlight,* http://www.libertylobby.org/articles/2001/20010313alaska_oil.html.

35. Boyd Graves, "The History of the Development of AIDS," http://www.boydgraves.com/timeline. See also, Joel Levy, "The Truth about AIDS," *The Little Book of Conspiracies* (Toronto: Key Porter Books), 14–15.

36. Final Call.com News, "AIDS Is Man-Made—Interview with Dr. Boyd Graves," *The Final Call,* October 5, 2004, http://www.finalcall.com/artman/publish/article_1597.shtml.

37. Jill Wolfson, "The World according to Mae," *The San Jose Mercury News,* March 28, 1982, http://www.maebrussell.com/Mae%20Brussell%20Articles/World%20According%20To%20Mae.html.

38. Michael Barkun, *A Culture of Conspiracy, Apocalyptic Visions in Contemporary America,* 4.

39. Jeffrey Bale, "'Conspiracy Theories' and Clandestine Politics," *Lobster* 29 (June 1995), http://www.lobster-magazine.co.uk/articles/l29consp.htm.

40. Dieter Groh, "The Temptation of Conspiracy Theory, or: Why Do Bad Things Happen to Good People? Part I: Preliminary Draft of a Theory of Conspiracy Theories," 3.

41. H. Lübbe, *Geschichtsbegriff und Geschichtsinteresse. Analytik und Pragmatik der Historie,* cited in Ibid.

42. Hannah Arendt, *The Human Condition* (Chicago: University of Chicago Press, 1958), 9, 247.

43. Ibid., 178.

44. See, for example, "Amazing $20 Dollar Bill 9/11 Coincidence," available at: http://www.allbrevard.net/_20bill/guest/, and a related story published on Glenn Beck's website, available at: http://archive.glennbeck.com/news/05172002.shtml.

45. Andrew Emerson, cited in "Amazing $20 Dollar Bill 9/11 Coincidence," available at: http://www.allbrevard.net/_20bill/guest/.

46. Matthew Gray, "Explaining Conspiracy Theories in Modern Arab Middle Eastern Political Discourse: Some Problems and Limitations of the Literature," *Critique: Critical Middle Eastern Studies,* Vol. 17, No. 2 (Summer 2008), 156.

47. "Under Fire, Obama Clarifies Support for Ground Zero Mosque," August 14, 2010, http://www.foxnews.com/politics/2010/08/14/obamas-support-ground-zero-mosque-draws.

48. Pew Research Center for People and the Press, "Growing Number of Americans Say Obama is a Muslim," August 19, 2010, http://people-press.org/report/645/.

49. For information and commentaries on this issue see, for example, "A Mosque at Ground Zero, Not Here, Not Ever," *The Daily Mail Online,* August 23, 2010, http://synonblog.dailymail.co.uk/2010/08/a-mosque-at-ground-zero-not-here-not-ever.html, "Under Fire, Obama Clarifies Support for Ground Zero Mosque,"

August 14, 2010, http://www.foxnews.com/politics/2010/08/14/obamas-support-ground-zero-mosque-draws, and Brad Knickerbocker, "'Ground Zero Mosque' Debate Hits the Streets of New York," *The Christian Science Monitor,* August 22, 2010, http://www.csmonitor.com/USA/2010/0822/Ground-Zero-mosque-debate-hits-the-streets-of-New-York.

50. David Aaronovitch, *Voodoo Histories, The Role of Conspiracy Theory in Shaping Modern History* (New York: Riverhead Books, 2010), 6.

51. Ibid.

52. Viren Swami, Tomas Chamorro-Premuzic, and Adrian Furnham, "Unanswered Questions: A Preliminary Investigation of Personality and Individual Difference Predictors of 9/11 Conspiracy Beliefs," *Applied Cognitive Psychology* (May 2009) 10.1002/acp 1583.

53. Ted Goertzel, "Belief in Conspiracy Theories," 739.

54. Ibid.

55. Richard Hofstadter, "The Paranoid Style in American Politics," *The Paranoid Style in American Politics, and Other Essays* (New York: Alfred A. Knopf, 1966), 4.

56. Ibid., 3–4.

57. Ibid., 4.

58. Nigel James, "Militias, the Patriot Movement, and the Internet: The Ideology of Conspiracism," in Jane Parish and Martin Parker, eds., *The Age of Anxiety* (Oxford: Blackwell, 2001), 83.

59. Thomas E. Flanagan, "The Politics of the Millennium," in Michael Barkun, ed., *Millennialism and Violence* (London: Frank Cass, 1996), 171.

60. Ted Goertzel, "Belief in Conspiracy Theories," 738–39.

61. See, for example, Anti-Defamation League, "Conspiracy Theories about Jews and 9/11 Cause Dangerous Mutations in Global Anti-Semitism," September 2, 2003, http://www.adl.org/presrele/asint_13/4346_13.htm.

62. United States Department of State, "The 4,000 Jews Rumor," April 28, 2009, http://www.america.gov/st/webchat-english/2009/April/20090430132244atlahtnevel4.020327e-02.html.

63. This analysis is considered by Matthew Dentith in his blog, "The Simplification Hypothesis," All Embracing, but Underwhelming, June 22, 2006, http://all-embracing.episto.org/2006/06/22/the-simplification-hypothesis/, and a series of comments on that post.

64. Dieter Groh, "The Temptation of Conspiracy Theory," 2.

65. Ibid.

66. Richard Hofstadter, "The Paranoid Style in American Politics," 37.

67. Nesta Webster, *Spacious Days* (London: Hutchinson and Company, 1950), 187.

68. Nesta Webster, *Secret Societies and Subversive Movements* (London: Boswell, 1924), 391–92.

69. Richard Hofstadter, "The Paranoid Style in American Politics," 29.

70. Carl Bernstein and Bob Woodward, "FBI Finds Nixon Aides Sabotaged Democrats," *The Washington Post*, October 10, 1972, p. AO1, http://www.washing tonpost.com/wp-dyn/content/article/2002/06/03/AR2005111001232.html.

71. George Johnson, *Architects of Fear, Conspiracy Theories and Paranoia in American Politics*, 15.

72. David Aaronovitch, *VooDoo Histories, The Role of Conspiracy Theory in Shaping Modern History*, 9.

73. Joyce Millman, "'The X-Files' Finds the Truth: Its Time Is Past," *The New York Times*, May 19, 2002, http://www.nytimes.com/2002/05/19/arts/television/19MILL.html?scp=1&sq=%22is%20the%20truth%20out%20there%22&st=cse.

74. See, for example, Michael Marek, "The X-Files Timeline," http://www.the mareks.com/xf/index.html.

75. Michelle Pauli, "Dan Brown's The Lost Symbol Breaks Records for First Week Sales," *The Guardian*, September 22, 2009, http://www.guardian.co.uk/books/2009/sep/22/dan-brown-lost-symbol-record-sales.

76. "The Da Vinci Code," May 6, 2006, http://www.rcdow.org.uk/davincicode/.

77. See, for example, Michael Barkun, *A Culture of Conspiracy, Apocalyptic Visions in Contemporary America*, and Mark Fenster, Conspiracy Theories, Secrecy and Power in American Culture (Minneapolis: University of Minnesota Press, 1999).

78. Michael Barkun, *A Culture of Conspiracy, Apocalyptic Visions in Contemporary America*, 20.

79. Jodi Dean, *Aliens in America: Conspiracy Cultures from Outerspace to Cyberspace* (Ithaca, NY: Cornell University Press, 1998), 8.

80. Ibid.

Chapter 2 The Big Three

1. J. M. Roberts, *The Mythology of the Secret Societies* (London: Secker and Warburg, 1972), vii.

2. Daniel Pipes, *Conspiracy, How the Paranoid Style Flourishes and Where it Comes From* (New York: The Free Press, 1997), 57–58.

3. Ibid.

4. Umberto Eco, *Foucault's Pendulum* (London: Picador, 1990), 375, cited in Daniel Pipes, *Conspiracy*, 58.

5. George Johnson, *Architects of Fear, Conspiracy Theories and Paranoia in American Politics*, 54.

6. Richard Hoagland, "The Twin Towers and the Great Masonic Experiments: Has the 'End of Days' Begun?" *Paranoia* (Spring 2002), cited and summarized by Michael Barkun, *A Culture of Conspiracy*, 160. Variations on this theory exist across

the Web. At www.theforbiddenknowledge.com, for example, the author outlines 11 ways in which the attacks on the World Trade Center are linked to the number 11. These include such numerological connections as: (1) September 11 is the 254th day of the year (and 2+5+4=11); (2) New York was the 11th state to join the Union; (3) Flight 11 had 92 people on board (9+2=11); and (4) Flight 77 had 65 people on board (6+5=11). In this view, Osama bin Laden was carrying out an Illuminati plan, in league with the American government, in order to bring the United States into a war that would destroy the economy and bring the world closer to the arrival of the Antichrist. "The Revelation: The World Trade Center September 11, 1001," www.theforbiddenknowledge.com/wtc/index02.htm.

7. Sovereign Great Priory of Canada, "Chivalry and Freemasonry," 2003, http://www.knightstemplar.ca/history/index.htm.

8. Alan Watt, *Transcript of the Dr. Bill Deagle Show,* June 11, 2007, http://www.alanwattsentientsentinel.eu/english/transcripts/Alan_Watt_on_BillDeagleShow_June112007.html.

9. Joel Levy, *The Little Book of Conspiracies,* 103.

10. The Covenant of the Islamic Resistance Movement (Hamas), August 18, 1988, http://www.mideastweb.org/hamas.htm.

11. J. T. Desaguliers, *The Constitutions of the Free-Masons containing the History, Charges, Regulations, etc. Of that now Ancient and Right Worshipful Fraternity. For the Use of the Lodges, London, 1723,* http://www.archive.org/stream/constitutionsoff00andeuoft#page/n19/mode/2up.

12. Ibid.

13. J. M. Roberts, *The Mythology of the Secret Societies,* 19.

14. James McConnachie and Robin Tudge, *The Rough Guide to Conspiracy Theories,* 77.

15. J. M. Roberts, *The Mythology of the Secret Societies,* 22, citing *Grand Lodge, 1717–1967* (Oxford: United Grand Lodge of England, 1967), 85, 88.

16. "The History of Freemasons' Hall," The United Grand Lodge of England, Available at: http://www.ugle.org.uk/ugle/the-history-of-freemasons-hall.htm. Today, in addition to hosting Masonic events, the Hall is used as a venue for occasions ranging from advertising campaigns to television and movie filming.

17. See, for example, The Masonic Service Association, "Masonic Membership Statistics," http://www.msana.com/msastats.asp.

18. For a fuller discussion of these ideas in the American context, see Martha F. Lee, *Earth First! Environmental Apocalypse* (Syracuse, NY: Syracuse University Press, 1995), 1.

19. Norman Davies, *Europe, A History* (London: Pimlico, 1997), 681.

20. J. M. Roberts, *The Mythology of the Secret Societies,* 19.

21. G. Johnson, *Architects of Fear, Conspiracy Theories and Paranoia in American Politics,* 36–37.

22. George Johnson's work is clear and concise, and especially thoughtful and reasonable on these points. Here, in particular, I am indebted to his analysis.

23. J. M. Roberts, *The Mythology of the Secret Societies*, 20.

24. G. Johnson, *Architects of Fear, Conspiracy Theories and Paranoia in American Politics*, 38.

25. Norman Davies, *Europe, A History*, 596–614.

26. James Billington, *Fire in the Minds of Men, Origins of the Revolutionary Faith* (New York: Basic Books, 1980), 92.

27. Manly P. Hall, *The Lost Keys of Freemasonry* (New York: Jeremy P. Tarcher, 2006), 69.

28. James Billington, *Fire in the Minds of Men, Origins of the Revolutionary Faith*, 92.

29. J. M. Roberts, *The Mythology of the Secret Societies*, 56.

30. Daniel Pipes, *Conspiracy, How the Paranoid Style Flourishes, and Where it Comes From*, 60.

31. J. T. Desaguliers, *The Constitutions of the Free-Masons containing the History, Charges, Regulations, etc. Of that now Ancient and Right Worshipful Fraternity. For the Use of the Lodges, London, 1723*, 50, http://www.archive.org/stream/constitutionsoff00andeuoft#page/n19/mode/2up.

32. Ibid.

33. J. M. Roberts, *The Mythology of the Secret Societies*, 57.

34. Manly P. Hall, *The Lost Keys of Freemasonry*, 13.

35. Cardinal Joseph Ratzinger, Congregation for the Doctrine of the Faith, "Declaration on Masonic Associations," November 26, 1983, http://www.vatican.va/roman_curia/congregations/cfaith/documents/rc_con_cfaith_doc_19831126_declaration-masonic_en.html.

36. "Reflections a Year after Declaration of Congregation for the Doctrine of the Faith, Irreconcilability between Christian Faith and Freemasonry," *L'Osservatore Romano*, March 11, 1985, http://www.vatican.va/roman_curia/congregations/cfaith/documents/rc_con_cfaith_doc_19850223_declaration-masonic_articolo_en.html.

37. Casanova, *Histoire de ma vie* (Paris: 1960), iii, 14.

38. J. M. Roberts, *The Mythology of the Secret Societies*, 42.

39. James Billington, *Fire in the Minds of Men, Origins of the Revolutionary Faith*, 92.

40. Thomas Flanagan, "Modernity and the Millennium: From Robespierre to Radical Feminism," in Martha F. Lee, ed., *Millennial Visions: Essays on Twentieth-Century Millenarianism* (Westport, CT: Praeger, 2000), 4–6.

41. See, for example, the discussions of this issue in Jacob L. Talmon, *The Origins of Totalitarian Democracy* (New York: Praeger, 1960), and Norman Davies, *Europe, A History*, 697–99.

42. Thomas Flanagan, "Modernity and the Millennium: From Robespierre to Radical Feminism," 5.

43. Ibid.

44. See, for example, Martha Lee and Herbert Simms, "American Millenarianism and Violence: Origins and Expressions," *Journal for the Study of Radicalism*, Volume 2, No. 2 (2008), 107–27.

45. Norman Davies, *Europe, A History,* 697–98.

46. James Billington, *Fire in the Minds of Men, Origins of the Revolutionary Faith,* 92–93.

47. Anthony Wallace, "Revitalization Movements," *American Anthropologist,* Volume 58 (1956), 264–81.

48. Ibid., 265.

49. Dan Brown, *The Lost Symbol* (New York: Doubleday, 2009), 31.

50. J. M. Roberts, *The Mythology of the Secret Societies,* 118.

51. René Le Forestier, *Les Illuminés de Bavière et la franc-maçonnerie allemande* (Geneva: Slatkine-Megariotis Reprints, 1974), 21.

52. J. M. Roberts, *The Mythology of the Secret Societies,* 119.

53. See, for example, "Knigge: Illuminati Weishaupt was a Jesuit in Disguise," http://troyspace2.wordpress.com/2008/09/16/knigge-illuminati-weishaupt-was-a-jesuit-in-disguise/.

54. J. M. Roberts, *The Mythology of the Secret Societies,* 119.

55. Nesta Webster, "The Illuminati," *Secret Societies and Subversive Movements* (London: Boswell, 1924), 198.

56. James Billington, *Fire in the Minds of Men, Origins of the Revolutionary Faith,* 94–95, and 126.

57. G. Johnson, *Architects of Fear, Conspiracy Theories and Paranoia in American Politics,* 43–47.

58. J. M. Roberts, *The Mythology of the Secret Societies,* 124.

59. G. Johnson, *Architects of Fear, Conspiracy Theories and Paranoia in American Politics,* 48.

60. See, for example, "History of the Illuminati," http://people.virginia.edu/~sfr/enam481/groupa/illumhist.html; "SMOKING GUN PROOF THAT ILLUMINATI PLAN TO ATTACK ON 9/11 AND BEYOND WAS WELL KNOWN AS FAR BACK AS 1995! Part 1—Future Cataclysmic Events Accurately Foretold In 1995 Illuminati Card Game—9/11 Attack Foreseen," http://www.cuttingedge.org/news/n1753.cfm; Wes Penre, "The Secret Order of the Illuminati, A Brief History of the Shadow Government," *The Illuminati News,* November 12, 1998, updated September 26, 2009, http://www.illuminati-news.com/moriah.htm#2.

61. Ibid.

62. See, for example, Michael Dargaville, "The Illuminati and the Galactic Federation," http://www.luisprada.com/Protected/the_illuminati_and_the_galactic_federation.htm.

63. Daniel Pipes, *Conspiracy, How the Paranoid Style Flourishes, and Where it Comes From*, 62–64.

64. J. M. Roberts, *The Mythology of the Secret Societies*, 123.

65. J. M. Roberts, *The Mythology of the Secret Societies*, 126.

66. See J. M. Roberts, *The Mythology of the Secret Societies*, 126, and G. Johnson, *Architects of Fear, Conspiracy Theories and Paranoia in American Politics*, 47–49.

67. See J. M. Roberts, *The Mythology of the Secret Societies*, 129, and G. Johnson, *Architects of Fear, Conspiracy Theories and Paranoia in American Politics*, 49–50. In addition, August W. Wolfstieg, *Bibliographie der FreimaurerischenLiteratur* (Leipzig, Germany: Verein Deutscher Freimaurer, 1911), a biography of literature concerning the Freemasons, discusses much of this material.

68. Bernard Bailyn, *The Ideological Origins of the American Revolution* (Cambridge, MA: Harvard University Press, 1992), 231–32.

69. James Billington, *Fire in the Minds of Men, Origins of the Revolutionary Faith*, 69.

Chapter 3   From Conspiracy to Superconspiracy, from Europe to America

1. Indeed, the Freemasons are anxious to claim John Locke as one of their own. See, for example, W. Bro. Alex Davidson, "The Masonic Concept of Liberty, Freemasonry and the Enlightenment," *Pietre-Stones Review of Freemasonry*, http://www.freemasons-freemasonry.com/Davidson.html.

2. John Locke, *Second Treatise on Government* (Indianapolis, IN: Hackett, 1980), 9.

3. Ibid., 52.

4. George Johnson, *Architects of Fear, Conspiracy Theories and Paranoia in American Politics*, 51.

5. James Billington, *Fire in the Minds of Men, Origins of the Revolutionary Faith*, 20.

6. Sisko Haiikala, "Denouncing the Enlightenment by Means of a Conspiracy Thesis, Göchhausen's Enthüllung der Weltbürgerrepublik," Translated by Pasi Ihalainen, http://www.jyu.fi/yhtfil/redescriptions/Yearbook%202000/Haikala%202000.pdf.

7. J. M. Roberts, *The Mythology of the Secret Societies*, 134.

8. Francis Parkman, *Montcalm and Wolfe*, Vol. 2 (Boston: Little, Brown, and Company, 1884), 285.

9. John Robison, *Proofs of a Conspiracy against All of the Religions and Governments of Europe*, Reprint (Whitefish, MT: Kessinger, 2003).

10. George Johnson, *Architects of Fear, Conspiracy Theories and Paranoia in American Politics*, 56.

11. Timothy Dwight, Sermon, cited in Vernon Stauffer, *New England and the Bavarian Illuminati* (PhD Dissertation, Columbia University, New York, 1918), 250–51, reprinted by Bibliobazaar. In *The Party of Fear,* Bennett traces the history of extreme right-wing politics in the United States. His examination finds that versions of the Illuminati conspiracy theory have been present in American political thought from the 1790s onward. David H. Bennett, *The Party of Fear, From Nativist Movements to the New Right in American History* (Chapel Hill: University of North Carolina Press, 1988).

12. Vernon Stauffer, *New England and the Bavarian Illuminati,* 360.

13. David Brion Davis, ed., *The Fear of Conspiracy: Images of Un-American Subversion from the Revolution to the Present* (Ithaca, NY: Cornell University Press, 1971), 23.

14. Peter Knight, "A Nation of Conspiracy Theorists," in Peter Knight, ed., *Conspiracy Nation: The Politics of Paranoia in Postwar America* (New York: New York University Press, 2002), 4.

15. George Grant, *Technology and Empire: Perspectives on North America* (Toronto: House of Anansi, 1969), 17.

16. Peter Knight, "A Nation of Conspiracy Theorists," 5.

17. While there is some dispute concerning Lady Queenborough's year of birth, it may be deduced from her age at the time of her marriage to Lord Queenborough. "American Girl to Marry Peer," *St. Petersburg Times,* July 16, 1921, 6.

18. Edith Starr Miller, *Common Sense in the Kitchen* (New York: Brentino's, 1918).

19. Lady Queenborough, Edith Starr Miller, *Occult Theocrasy.* Reprint of the 1933 edition (Palmdale, CA: Christian Book Club of America, 1976).

20. Ibid., 8.

21. Ibid., 9–10.

22. "Lord Queensborough [*sic*] Married to Edith Starr Miller." *Pittsburgh Gazette-Times,* July 20, 1921, 2.

23. See, for example, Andrew Marr, *A History of Modern Britain* (London: MacMillan, 2007), 40–42, and David Cannadine, *In Churchill's Shadow, Confronting the Past in Modern Britain* (Oxford: Oxford University Press, 2003), 11–18.

24. Lady Queenborough, Edith Starr Miller, *Occult Theocrasy,* 661.

25. Ibid., 662.

26. Michael Barkun, *A Culture of Conspiracy, Apocalyptic Visions in Contemporary America,* 48–49.

27. See, for example, "Russia: World's Leader in State Sponsored Terrorism!!!" *Newswatch Magazine,* July 1, 2002, http://newswatchmagazine.org/julyaug 02/julyaug02.htm, or Don Marquis, "Former Illuminist Witch Reveals Strong Witchcraft Ties to Freemasonry," http://letsrollforums.com/kurt-cobain-mind-control-t17443p30.html?s=16e58c34074dd73bcfc5accf80a25927&

28. Pat Robertson, *The New World Order* (Dallas, TX: Word Publishing, 1991). See especially 71, 180–81.

29. Kellene Bishop, "What Would You Do to Stop Hitler Today?" http://kellene bishop.wordpress.com/.

30. Martin Durham, *The Christian Right: The Far Right and the Boundaries of American Conservatism* (Manchester, UK: Manchester University Press, 2000), 134.

31. See, for example, Islamic Party of Britain, "Satanic Voices." March 26, 2003, http://www.islamicparty.com/satvoices/acknowledgements.htm.

32. Nesta Webster, *Spacious Days,* 11–13. Some material from the above section is reprinted from Martha Lee, "Nesta Webster: The Voice of Conspiracy," *Journal of Women's History,* Vol. 17, No. 3 (2005), 81–104.

33. Nesta Webster, *Spacious Days,* 32–37.

34. Ibid., 36.

35. Ibid., 58, 59.

36. Ibid., 84.

37. Ibid., 103.

38. Webster notes that 20 years after her visit, "agitators" spread unrest in Burma: "With such diabolical cunning do the agents of world unrest set about their work!" Ibid., 112, 113.

39. Ibid., 112.

40. Ibid., 149, and Richard Gilman, *Behind World Revolution, The Strange Case of Nesta Webster* (Ann Arbor, MI: Insights Books, 1982), 65.

41. Nesta Webster, *Spacious Days,* 166.

42. Nesta Webster, *The Sheep Track* (London: John Murray, 1924), 442.

43. Seneca, cited in Ibid., 442.

44. "The Sheep Track," *New York Times,* March 16, 1919, 137. See also, Lucian Cary, "Recent Fiction," *The Dial,* August 16, 1914, 107; "The Sheep Track," *The Spectator,* April 11, 1913, 617; "The Sheep Track," *New York Times,* August 16, 1914, 346; and "The Sheep Track," *The Bookman* (1914), 94–95.

45. Nesta Webster, *Britain's Call to Arms, An Appeal to Our Women* (London: Hugh Rees, 1914), 4–5.

46. Ibid., 14.

47. Nesta Webster, "Women and Civilisation," *The Nineteenth Century and After,* Volume 88, Number 525 (November 1920), 750.

48. Ibid., 754.

49. Ibid., 759.

50. See, for example, Oliver Willis, "Liberal Elitism? No. Some People are, Sadly, Stupid," *The Huffington Post,* August 28, 2010, http://www.huffingtonpost.com/oli ver-willis/liberal-elitism-no-some-p_b_356218.html. Recent research tests the link between level of education and conspiracy belief (see, for example, Anita Waters,

"Conspiracy Theories as Ethnosociologies: Explanation and Intention in African American Political Culture," *Journal of Black Studies*, Vol. 28, No. 1 [1997], 112–25). It suggests this link is unsupported by data.

51. Nesta Webster, *Spacious Days*, 171.

52. She was, however, unwilling to conclude that was the only possible reason for her familiarity with prerevolutionary France. Webster had great sympathy for theories of extrasensory perception and suggests that it might also be the result of ancestral memory (her grandfather might have known of it, or her mother might have read about France while pregnant with Nesta) or might even have been "conveyed from the minds of those who have passed over," "*spirit presences*" around us, or even of those still living on the earth [emphasis in original]."

53. Richard Gilman, *Behind World Revolution*, 32. In her review of *Louis XVI and Marie Antoinette before the Revolution*, Gertrude Bagley also notes that Webster's Chevalier was a "best-seller." Gertrude Bagley, "Nearing the End of the Bourbons," *Boston Evening Transcript*, April 16, 1938, 2.

54. Thurlow compares Webster's skills to those of Lady Antonia Fraser. Richard Thurlow, "The Powers of Darkness, Conspiracy Belief and Political Strategy," *Patterns of Prejudice* Vol. 12, No. 6 (Nov.-Dec. 1978), 11.

55. Nesta Webster, *Spacious Days*, 185, 187.

56. Sidney B. Fay, "The French Revolution," *The American Political Science Review*, Vol. 14 (1920), 732–33.

57. "The people may make riots, but never revolutions." Webster quotes le Bon's *Psychologie des Revolutions*. Nesta Webster, *Spacious Days*, 187.

58. Nesta Webster, *The French Revolution, A Study in Democracy* (London: Constable, 1926), 8.

59. Nesta Webster, *Spacious Days*, 187.

60. Webster would likely have been pleased by both remarks. Fred Fling, "The French Revolution," *The American Historical Review*, Vol. 25, 714. Sidney B. Fay, "The French Revolution, *American Political Science Review*, Vol. 14, 733.

61. Nesta Webster, *The Past History of the World Revolution*, Lecture delivered at the Royal Artillery Institution, Woolwich, Tuesday, Nov. 30, 1920 (Royal Artillery Institution Printing House, 1921), 468–70, 473–74.

62. Nesta Webster, *World Revolution, The Plot against Civilization* (London: Constable and Company, 1921), viii.

63. Ibid.

64. Nesta Webster, "Illuminism and the World Revolution," *The Nineteenth Century and After*, Vol. 88 (July–December 1920), 97–99.

65. Nesta Webster, *World Revolution*, viii.

66. Ibid., 327.

67. Nesta Webster, *Secret Societies and Subversive Movements*, v.

68. See, for example, "Thy Weapon of War," a blog providing anti-Semitic information and sources for its readers, http://thy-weapon-of-war.blogspot.com/.

69. Nesta Webster, *Secret Societies and Subversive Movements*, 369.

70. Ibid., 373.

71. Ibid., 391–92.

72. Ibid., 399.

73. Ibid., 400.

74. Webster suggests that if one power controls the rest, it is the Pan-German Power, the Jewish Power, or Illuminism. She concludes that it might be the Germans and Jews working through a secret inner circle within the Illuminati. If this is so, she hypothesizes that the Germans (who hope to destroy the Allies) may be working with the Jews (who hope to destroy Christian civilization). A second possible scenario is that the hidden center of power consists solely of Jews, who are using both the Pan-Germans and the Gentile Illuminati as their tools. Ibid., 401, 403.

75. Ibid., 404.

76. Colin Holmes, *Anti-Semitism in British Society, 1876–1939* (London: Edward Arnold, 1979), 229.

77. Winston Churchill, "Zionism versus Bolshevism, A Struggle for the Soul of the Jewish People," *Illustrated Sunday Herald,* February 8, 1920, 5.

78. See, for example, the cover story, "The Progress of World Revolution," *The Patriot*, Vol. 9, No. 191 (October 1, 1925), 457–58. Advertisements for her books were often included in the paper.

79. Martin Durham, *Women and Fascism* (London: Routledge, 1998), 27. The British Fascists Ltd. was originally the British Fascisti; it changed its name in May 1924. Julie Gottlieb, *Feminine Fascism, Women in Britain's Fascist Movement* (London: I. B. Taurus, 2003), 21–22.

80. Gottlieb notes that women in the British Fascists tended to have similar backgrounds. They were of the middle and upper classes; many had served in the military, had a role in administering the Empire, and had landed status. A number were also titled. Julie Gottlieb, *Feminine Fascism, Women in Britain's Fascist Movement*, 30–31.

81. Barbara Storm Farr, *The Development and Impact of Right-Wing Politics in Britain, 1903–1932* (New York: Garland, 1987), 76.

82. See, for example, "Mrs. Nesta H. Webster on Fascism," *The British Lion*, January 7, 1927, 7.

83. Nesta Webster, "The Patriots' Inquiry Centre," Correspondence, *The Patriot*, October 20, 1927, 382. The same issue welcomes Mrs. Webster to the ranks of British Fascism. The Fascisti party was not long-lived. Gottlieb and Durham argue that it inevitably failed because it had no viable leader and because its platform was not fully fascist. See Durham, 27 and Gottlieb, 34.

84. *The Daily Telegraph,* November 19, 1927.

85. Markku Ruotsila, "Mrs. Webster's Religion: Conspiracist Extremism on the Christian Far Right," *Patterns of Prejudice,* Vol. 38, No. 2 (2004), 122.

86. Nesta Webster, "Where Are We Going?" Part 1, "Socialist Dreams," *The Patriot,* January 9, 1947.

87. Nesta Webster [Julian Sterne], *The Secret of the Zodiac* (London: Boswell, 1933), 73.

88. Ibid.

89. They were followed by another journal article in *The Nineteenth Century and After,* "Marie Antoinette, A Slandered Queen."

90. See, for example, Katherine Woods, "Marie Antoinette and Louis XVI before the Revolution," *New York Times Book Review,* January 16, 1938, 9, and Alan Taylor, "Two Biographies," *The Manchester Guardian,* Nov. 13, 1936, 7.

91. Nesta Webster, *Germany and England* (London: Boswell, 1938), 15.

92. Ibid., 46–47.

93. Ibid., 25.

94. Ibid., 34.

95. *Isle of Wight County Press,* April 25, 1942, cited in R. Gilman, *Behind World Revolution,* 51.

96. S. L., "Mrs. Nesta Webster, Studies in French History." Obituary. *The Times,* May 18, 1960, 17. The revised sixth edition of *World Revolution* appeared in 1960. It was edited by Anthony Gittens, however, not Webster.

97. Serge Moscovici, "The Conspiracy Mentality," in C. F. Graumann and S. Moscovici, eds., *Changing Conceptions of Conspiracy* (London: Springer-Verlag, 1987), 157.

98. See, for example, Cynthia Enloe, *Bananas, Beaches and Bases* (Berkeley: University of California Press, 1989), 61–64.

Chapter 4 Conspiracy in America?

1. George Modelski, "Long Cycles in Global Politics," https://faculty.washing ton.edu/modelski/LCGPeolss.htm.

2. Ibid.

3. Ibid.

4. Immanuel Wallerstein, "The Three Instances of Hegemony in the Capitalist World-Economy," *The Politics of the World Economy, Essays by Immanuel Wallerstein* (Cambridge: Cambridge University Press, 1984), 38–39.

5. Ibid., 39.

6. Ibid.,40.

7. Richard Rosecrance summarizes a number of these theories in a review of a number of long-cycle books, including monographs by Joshua Goldstein,

Nikolai Kondratieff, and George Modelski. Richard Rosecrance, "Long Cycle Theory in International Relations," *International Organization*, Vol. 41, No. 2 (1987), 283–301.

8. Andrew Marr, *A History of Modern Britain*, 36.

9. Ibid., 9.

10. Nesta H. Webster, *Secret Societies and Subversive Movements*, 401.

11. See, for example, Nesta H. Webster, *World Revolution, the Plot against Civilization*, Schematic Diagram of Conspiracy, xiii, and Nesta H. Webster, *Secret Societies and Subversive Movements*.

12. Nesta H. Webster, *Secret Societies and Subversive Movements*, 336.

13. Ibid.

14. Ibid.

15. William Faulkner, "Banquet Speech," Nobelprize.org, http://nobelprize.org/nobel_prizes/literature/laureates/1949/faulkner-speech.html.

16. Richard Fried, *Nightmare in Red, The McCarthy Era in Perspective* (New York: Oxford University Press, 1991), 6.

17. Robert Welch, *The Blue Book of the John Birch Society* (Appleton, WI: Western Islands Publishers, 2000), 149.

18. Ibid., 1–32.

19. Ibid., 20.

20. Ibid., 19.

21. M. Barkun, *A Culture of Conspiracy, Apocalyptic Visions in Contemporary Culture*, 49.

22. Stephen E. Atkins, *Holocaust Denial as an International Movement* (Westport, CT: Praeger, 2009), 155–56.

23. Revilo P. Oliver, "A Centennial You Should Notice," Article reprinted from *The Liberty Bell*, December 1988, http://www.revilo-oliver.com/rpo/Centennial.html.

24. R. Gilman, *Behind World Revolution, The Strange Case of Nesta Webster*, 53.

25. Jeffrey Kaplan, ed., *The Encyclopedia of White Power, A Sourcebook on the Racist Right* (Walnut Creek, CA: Altamira Press), 347. See also Gerald Winrod, *The Truth about the Protocols*, available at: http://www.biblebelievers.org.au/truth.htm, which makes this argument in his own words.

26. Revilo P. Oliver, "Conspiracy or Degeneracy," Speech to the New England Rally for God, Family, and Country," Boston, 1966., cited in Sara Diamond, *Roads to Dominion: Right Wing Movements and Political Power in the United States* (New York: Guilford Press, 1995), 361. Full audio recording is available at: revilo–oliver.com: http://www.revilo-oliver.com/news/1966/07/conspiracy-or-degeneracy/.   Oliver himself points out that the remark in question was made in the context of an argument that eliminating various groups (the Illuminati, Communists, and Jews) would not lead to a perfect world. At the same time, however, he clearly identifies a

world where this could happen as desirable. See, for example, Revilo Oliver, "Contemporary Journalists," available at: http://www.revilo-oliver.com/rpo/Contemporary_Journalists.html. The article is taken from *The Liberty Bell*, February 1985.

27. Robert Welch, *The Blue Book of the John Birch Society*, 60.

28. Ibid., 43.

29. See, for example, John Broyles, *The John Birch Society: Anatomy of a Protest* (Boston: Beacon Press, 1964), cited in "The John Birch Society," Political Research Associates, available at: http://www.publiceye.org/tooclose/jbs.html.

30. Barbara Stone, "The John Birch Society: A Profile," *The Journal of Politics*, Vol. 36, No. 1 (Feb. 1974), 195.

31. Ibid., 196.

32. Alan F. Westin, "The John Birch Society: 'Radical Right' and 'Extreme Left' in the Political Context of Post World War Two (1962)" in Daniel Bell, *The Radical Right*, 3rd ed. (New Brunswick, NJ: Transaction Publishers, 2001).

33. Ibid., 242.

34. Ibid., 239.

35. Ibid.

36. See, for example, Revilo Oliver, "Marxmanship in Dallas [Part II]," American *Opinion*, Vol. 7, No. 3 (March 1964), 65–78. Reprinted at: http://www.kenrahn.com/jfk/the_critics/oliver/marxmanship_in_dallas_ii.html.

37. Robert Welch, "The Truth in Time," reprinted in *The Blue Book of the John Birch Society*, 173. The article was originally printed in *American Opinion*, Vol. 9, No. 10, 1–26.

38. Robert Welch, "The Truth in Time," 173.

39. Ibid.

40. Ibid., 171–73 and 196–97.

41. Ibid., 172.

42. Ibid.

43. Ibid., 194.

44. Ibid., 196.

45. James T. Patterson, *Grand Expectations: the United States, 1945–74* (Oxford: Oxford University Press, 1997), 449.

46. Federal Bureau of Investigation, "The F.B.I.: A Centennial History, 1908–2008," http://www.fbi.gov/fbihistorybook.htm#chapter4.

47. Select Committee to Study Governmental Operations with Respect to Intelligence Activities, United States Senate, "Intelligence Activities and the Rights of Americans," http://www.icdc.com/~paulwolf/cointelpro/churchfinalreportIIb.htm.

48. See, for example, "Above the Law," *The Washington Post Times Herald*, April 22, 1966, A20.

49. Nicholas M. Horrock, "80 Institutions Used in C.I.A. Mind Studies," *New York Times*, August 4, 1977, 17.

50. Nicholas M. Horrock, "238 Break-Ins Committed by F.B.I. over 26 Years," *New York Times*, September 26, 1975, 77.

51. Seymour M. Hersh, "Underground for the C.I.A. in New York: An Ex-Agent Tells of Spying on Students," *The New York Times*, December 29, 1974, 1.

52. John M. Crewdson, "C.I.A. Secretly Owned Insurance Complex and Invested Profits in Stock Market," *The New York Times*, April 27, 1976, 25.

53. Ibid.

54. Joseph Kraft, "Developing a 'Gullibility Gap,'" *The Washington Post*, January 23, 1975, A23.

55. Ibid.

56. Daniel Pipes, *Conspiracy—How the Paranoid Style Flourishes and Where it Comes From*, 116.

57. George H. W. Bush, "Address before a Joint Session of the Congress on the Cessation of the Persian Gulf Conflict," March 6, 1991, George Bush Presidential Library and Museum, http://bushlibrary.tamu.edu/research/public_papers.php?id=2767&year=1991&month=3.

58. Michael Barkun, *A Culture of Conspiracy, Apocalyptic Visions in Contemporary America*, 39–40.

59. Ibid., 39.

60. Julian Sterne [Nesta Webster], *The Secret of the Zodiac*.

61. Robert Welch, cited in G. Edward Griffin, *The Life and Words of Robert Welch, Founder of the John Birch Society* (Thousand Oaks, CA: American Media, 1975), 226.

62. G. Johnson, *Architects of Fear, Conspiracy Theories and Paranoia in American Politics*, 137–38. See also Howard Spier, " 'Zionists and Freemasons' in Soviet Propaganda," *Patterns of Prejudice*, Vol. 13, No. 1 (1979), 1–5.

63. Daneen Peterson, "About the NAU—What You Don't Know CAN Hurt You," Speech, Washington D.C., June 15, 2007, http://www.stopthenorthamericanunion.com/WhatYouDontKnow.html.

64. Alan Barth, "Report on the Rampageous Right," *The New York Times Sunday Magazine*, November 26, 1961, 25, 130–31. This article, along with "Thunder against the Right," *Time*, November 24, 1961, is cited by Lee Edwards in *Conservative Revolution, The Movement That Remade America* (New York: Free Press, 1999) as key to this process.

65. William Buckley, cited in Niels Bjerre-Poulson, *Right Face, Organizing the American Conservative Movement, 1945–1965* (Copenhagen: Museum Tusculanum Press, 2002), 206.

66. Niels Bjerre-Poulson, *Right Face, Organizing the American Conservative Movement, 1945–1965*, 207.

67. Lee Edwards, *Conservative Revolution, The Movement That Remade America*, 107.

68. Ibid.

69. George Modelski, "Long Cycles in Global Politics," https://faculty.washing ton.edu/modelski/LCGPeolss.htm.

70. Ibid.

71. Immanuel Wallerstein, "The Three Instances of Hegemony in the Capitalist World-Economy," 40.

72. Ibid.

73. Ibid., 46.

74. Immanuel Wallerstein, "America and the World: The Twin Towers as Metaphor," Charles R. Lawrence II Memorial Lecture, Brooklyn College, Dec. 5, 2001, Social Science Research Council, http://essays.ssrc.org/sept11/essays/wallerstein.htm.

75. Ibid.

76. Immanuel Wallerstein, "The Three Instances of Hegemony in the Capitalist World-Economy," 46.

77. Ronald Reagan most famously used this term in his speech to the British Parliament on June 8, 1982, when he asked "Must freedom wither in a quiet, deadening accommodation with totalitarian evil?" The sentiment behind it, however, was generated decades earlier, http://www.reagan.utexas.edu/archives/speeches/1982/60882a.htm.

78. Thomas Flanagan, "The Politics of the Millennium," in Michael Barkun, ed., *Millennialism and Violence,* 171.

79. "President Zachary Taylor Just Plain Died in Office," *Albany Times Union,* June 27, 1991, http://www.highbeam.com/doc/1G1–156232096.html.

80. Charles Krauthammer, "A Rash of Conspiracy Theories; When Do We Dig Up Bill Casey?" *The Washington Post,* July 5, 1991, http://www.highbeam.com/doc/1P2–1073359.html.

81. "Next Up: Who Killed Huey?" *Chicago Sun-Times,* http://www.highbeam.com/doc/1P2–4060854.html.

82. "PAPERBACK BEST SELLERS: January 20, 1991—New York Times," *The New York Times,* http://www.highbeam.com/doc/1S1–9199101200004091.html.

83. Clifford Krauss, "28 Years After Kennedy's Assassination, Conspiracy Theories Refuse to Die," *The New York Times,* January 5, 1992, http://www.nytimes.com/1992/01/05/us/28-years-after-kennedy-s-assassination-conspiracy-theories-refuse-to-die.html.

84. Charles Krauthammer, "A Rash of Conspiracy Theories; When Do We Dig Up Bill Casey?" *The Washington Post,* July 5, 1991, http://www.highbeam.com/doc/1P2–1073359.html.

85. Ibid.

86. George Bush, Address before a Joint Session of the Congress on the Persian Gulf Crisis and the Federal Budget Deficit, September 11, 1990, http://bushlibrary.tamu.edu/research/public_papers.php?id=2217&year=1990&month=9.

87. Pat Robertson, *The New World Order.* See especially 71, 180–81.

88. Gustav Niebuhr, "Pat Robertston Says He Intended No Anti-Semitism in Book He Wrote Four Years Ago," *The New York Times,* March 4, 1995, http://www.nytimes.com/1995/03/04/us/pat-robertston-says-he-intended-no-anti-semitism-in-book-he-wrote-four-years-ago.html?scp=9&sq=.

89. Pat Robertson, *The New World Order,* xi.

90. Michael Barkun, *A Culture of Conspiracy, Apocalyptic Visions in Contemporary America,* 53.

91. Pat Robertson, *The New World Order,* 37.

92. Gustav Niebuhr, "Pat Robertston Says He Intended No Anti-Semitism in Book He Wrote Four Years Ago," *The New York Times,* March 4, 1995, http://www.nytimes.com/1995/03/04/us/pat-robertston-says-he-intended-no-anti-semitism-in-book-he-wrote-four-years-ago.html?scp=9&sq=.

93. For an explanation of these points, see Barbara Brasher, "When Your Friend is Your Enemy, American Christian Fundamentalists and Israel at the New Millennium," in Martha F. Lee, ed., *Millennial Visions* (Westport, CT: Praeger, 2000), 135–47.

Chapter 5 9/11

1. Mark Fenster, cited in Thomas Hargrove, "Third of Americans Suspect 9–11 Government Conspiracy," Scripps News, August 1, 2006, http://www.scrippsnews.com/911poll.

2. Thomas Hargrove, "Third of Americans Suspect 9–11 Government Conspiracy," Scripps News, August 1, 2006, http://www.scrippsnews.com/911poll.

3. "911Truth.org: An Overview," August 26, 2004, http://www.911truth.org/article.php?story=20061014120445472#mission.

4. Janice Matthews, cited in Thomas Hargrove, "Third of Americans Suspect 9–11 Government Conspiracy," Scripps News, August 1, 2006, http://www.scrippsnews.com/911poll.

5. *Loose Change* Fact Sheet, *Loose Change* 9/11, An American Coup, http://www.loosechange911.com/about/faq/.

6. Program on International Policy Attitudes, University of Maryland, "International Poll: No Consensus on Who was Behind 9/11," http://www.worldpublicopinion.org/pipa/articles/international_security_bt/535.php?nid=&id=&pnt=535. Interviews were conducted in China, Indonesia, Russia, Egypt, France, Germany, Great Britain, Italy, Jordan, Kenya, Mexico, the Palestinian Territories, South Korea, Taiwan, Turkey, and the Ukraine, and 16,063 individuals were surveyed between July 15 and August 31, 2008. The margins of error for these surveys range from +/− 3 to 4 percent.

7. Program on International Policy Attitudes, University of Maryland, "International Poll: No Consensus on Who was Behind 9/11," http://www.world publicopinion.org/pipa/articles/international_security_bt/535.php?nid=&id=&pnt=535.

8. Ibid.

9. Michael Cox, "Whatever Happened to American Decline? International Relations and the New United States Hegemony," *New Political Economy,* Vol. 6, No. 3 (2001), 315.

10. Stephen Gill, "The Global Organic Crisis: Paradoxes, Dangers, and Opportunities," *Monthly Review Magazine,* February 15, 2010, http://mrzine.monthly review.org/2010/gill150210.html#_edn6.

11. Stephen Gill, "Gramsci, Modernity and Globalization," International Gramsci Society, January 2003, http://www.internationalgramscisociety.org/resources/online_articles/articles/gill01.shtml.

12. Michael Cox, "Whatever Happened to American Decline? International Relations and the New United States Hegemony," 323–27.

13. Stephen Gill, "The Global Organic Crisis: Paradoxes, Dangers, and Opportunities."

14. See Michael Cox, "Whatever Happened to American Decline? International Relations and the New United States Hegemony," for an excellent summation of these arguments.

15. Mary Kaldor, *New and Old Wars,* 2nd ed. (Palo Alto, CA: Stanford University Press, 2007), 107.

16. Adam Roberts, "Lives and Statistics: Are 90% of War Victims Civilians?" *Survival,* Vol. 52, No. 3 (2010), 116.

17. See, for example, International Committee of the Red Cross, "Protocol Additional to the Geneva Conventions of 12 August 1949, and relating to the Protection of Victims of International Armed Conflicts (Protocol I)," June 8, 1977, http://www.icrc.org/ihl.nsf/COM/470–750042?OpenDocument.

18. Edward S. Cohen, *The Politics of Globalization in the United States* (Washington, D.C.: Georgetown University Press, 2001), 4.

19. Robert B. Reich, *The Work of Nations* (Toronto: Random House, 1992), 172.

20. Gabriel Weimann, "How Modern Terrorism Uses the Internet," United States Institute of Peace, Special Report 116, March 2004, http://www.usip.org/files/resources/sr116.pdf, 5.

21. Donald Rumsfeld, "Web Site OPSEC Discrepancies," United States Government Department of Defense, January 14, 2003, http://www.defense.gov/webmasters/policy/rumsfeld_memo_to_DOD_webmasters.html.

22. Gabriel Weimann, "How Modern Terrorism Uses the Internet," United States Institute of Peace, Special Report 116, March 2004, http://www.usip.org/files/resources/sr116.pdf, 6.

23. Lee Sproull and Sara Kiesler, *Connections, New Ways of Working in the Net-worked Organization* (Boston: MIT Press, 1992), 15.

24. Gabriel Weimann, "How Modern Terrorism Uses the Internet," United States Institute of Peace, Special Report 116, March 2004, http://www.usip.org/files/resources/sr116.pdf, 9.

25. Ibid.

26. Barry Cooper, *New Political Religions, or an Analysis of Modern Terrorism* (Columbia: University of Missouri Press, 2005), 174.

27. For a fascinating examination of the network that was involved in the September 11, 2001, attacks, including several graphical representations of their connections, see Valdis E. Krebs, "Uncloaking Terrorist Networks," *First Monday,* Vol. 7, No. 4 (April 2002), http://firstmonday.org/htbin/cgiwrap/bin/ojs/index.php/fm/article/view/941/863.

28. Kathryn Olmsted, *Real Enemies, Conspiracy Theories and American Democracy, World War 1 to 9/11* (Oxford: Oxford University Press, 2009), 5.

29. See, for example, Peter Allen, "Marion Cotillard's 9/11 Conspiracy Theory," *The Daily Telegraph,* March 1, 2008, http://www.telegraph.co.uk/news/worldnews/1580414/Marion-Cotillards-911-conspiracy-theory.html.

30. Anti-Defamation League, "Unravelling Anti-Semitic 9/11 Conspiracy Theories," 2003, http://www.adl.org/anti_semitism/9–11conspiracytheories.pdf.

31. Ibid.

32. Martin J. Manning and Herbert Romerstein, *Historical Dictionary of American Propaganda* (Westport, CT: Greenwood Publishing, 2004), 277.

33. Anti-Defamation League, "Unravelling Anti-Semitic 9/11 Conspiracy Theories," 2003, http://www.adl.org/anti_semitism/9–11conspiracytheories.pdf.

34. Ibid.

35. Thomas Hobbes, *Leviathan* (Indianapolis, IN: Hackett Publishing, 1994), 31.

36. "The World Trade Center, September 11, 2001," The Revelation, http://www.theforbiddenknowledge.com/wtc/index02.htm.

37. Ibid.

38. Further examination of numerological data and the events of September 11 can be found at a number of websites, including: "9/11 Numerology and Symbology, http://www.bibliotecapleyades.net/sociopolitica/atlantean_conspiracy/atlantean_conspiracy40.htm, and "9/11 Numerology—Undeniable Proof that 9/11 & War on Terror are Secret Society NWO Creations," http://www.abovetopsecret.com/forum/thread337330/pg1/.

39. Mark Fenster, *Conspiracy Theories: Secrecy and Power in American Culture,* xvi.

40. Kathryn S. Olmsted, *Real Enemies, Conspiracy Theories and American Democracy, World War 1 to 9/11,* 8.

41. Ibid., 6–9.

42. Joseph Mercola, "Airport Scanners: Radiation is *Not* the Only Health Hazard," *The Huffington Post,* December 15, 2010, http://www.huffingtonpost.com/dr-mercola/airport-scanners-how-much-radiation-_b_793071.html.

Chapter 6 Extremism and Apathy

1. Ray Pratt, "Theorizing Conspiracy," *Theory and Society,* Vol. 32, No. 2 (Apr. 2003), 258.

2. See, for example, Ted Goertzel, "Belief in Conspiracy Theories," 731–42, and Marina Abalakina-Paap et al., "Beliefs in Conspiracies," 637–47.

3. Marina Abalakina-Paap et al., "Beliefs in Conspiracies," 645.

4. Centers for Disease Control and Prevention, "U.S. Public Health Service Study at Tuskegee, Tuskegee Timeline," http://www.cdc.gov/tuskegee/timeline.htm.

5. Anita Waters, "Conspiracy Theories as Ethnosociologies: Explanation and Intention in African American Political Culture," 121. Waters's survey sample was of adults over the age of 18 in New York City. The total number of cases was 1,047, of which 408 were African American.

6. Anita Waters, "Conspiracy Theories as Ethnosociologies: Explanation and Intention in African American Political Culture," 121–22.

7. Ibid., 120.

8. Matthew Gray, "Explaining Conspiracy Theories in modern Arab Middle Eastern Political Discourse: Some Problems and Limitations of the Literature," 165.

9. For this pithy way of describing the issue, I am indebted to Jeffrey Bale, "Conspiracy Theories and Clandestine Politics," Lobster 29 (1995), http://www.lobster-magazine.co.uk/articles/l29consp.htm.

10. Richard Hofstadter, "The Paranoid Style in American Politics," 4.

11. Robert Young, "Fundamentalism and Terrorism," in Jerry S. Piven, Paul Ziolo, and Henry W. Lawton, eds., *Terror and Apocalypse: Psychological Undercurrents of History,* Vol. 2 (Lincoln, NE: IUniverse, 2002), 210.

12. Charles B. Strozier and Katharine Boyd, "The Psychology of Apocalypticism," *The Journal of Psychohistory,* Vol. 37, No. 4 (Spring 2010), 284.

13. Thomas E. Flanagan, "The Politics of the Millennium," 173.

14. James Stenzel, "Dumping Goy Politics," *The Jew Watch,* http://www.jewwatch.com/jew-worldconspiracies-illuminati.html.

15. Team Infinity, "Oklahoma City Bombing Questions Demand an Answer," http://www.stopcovertwar.com/McVeigh.html.

16. Jon Ronson, "Conspirators," *The Guardian,* May 5, 2001, http://www.guardian.co.uk/world/2001/may/05/mcveigh.usa.

17. Walter Laqueur, *The Changing Face of Anti-Semitism, From Ancient Times to the Present Day,* 95.

18. Ibid., 95–96.

19. Albert S. Lindemann, Anti-Semitism before the Holocaust (Harlow, England: Pearson, 2000), 52.

20. Nesta Webster, *Secret Societies and Subversive Movements*, 374.

21. Ibid.

22. Ibid.

23. Ibid., 408.

24. Nesta Webster, *World Revolution, The Plot against Civilization*.

25. Ibid., 305.

26. See, for example, Daniel Pipes, Index, *Conspiracy, How the Paranoid Style Flourishes and Where It Comes From*, 238 and 241. Pipes's book contains a detailed discussion of this issue.

27. Andrew MacDonald, *The Turner Diaries*, http://www.jrbooksonline.com/PDF_Books/TurnerDiaries.pdf.

28. Camille Jackson, "Fightin' Words," *Intelligence Report*, Vol. 15 (Fall 2004), Southern Poverty Law Center, http://www.splcenter.org/get-informed/intelligence-report/browse-all-issues/2004/fall/fightin-words.

29. This definition is drawn from Yonina Talmon, "Millenarism," *Encyclopedia of the Social Sciences*, Vol. 10 (New York: MacMillan, 1968), 351.

30. Thomas Flanagan, "The Politics of the Millennium," 173.

31. Mark Fenster, *Conspiracy Theories, Secrecy and Power in American Culture*, 147.

32. Ibid., 175.

33. Dr. Jack and Rexella Van Impe, "Final World Government, When, Now?" http://www.jvim.org/pt/2004/2004SeptOct.pdf.

34. Joanna Sweet and Martha Lee, "Christian Exodus: A Modern American Millenarian Movement," *Journal for the Study of Radicalism*, Vol. 4, No. 1 (2010), 11.

35. Cory Burnell, cited in Joanna Sweet and Martha Lee, "Christian Exodus: A Modern American Millenarian Movement," *Journal for the Study of Radicalism*, Vol. 4, No. 1 (2010), 11.

36. Ibid.

37. Michael Barkun, *A Culture of Conspiracy, Apocalyptic Visions in Contemporary America*, 169.

38. Catherine Wessinger's *Millennialism, Persecution and Violence* provides an excellent analysis of the effects of persecution on a range of millenarian movements. For these cases, see Ian Reader, "Imagined Persecution, Aum Shinrikyo, Millennialism, and the Legitimation of Violence," in Catherine Wessinger, ed., *Millennialism, Persecution and Violence* (Syracuse, NY: Syracuse University Press, 2000), 158–82, and Rebecca Moore, "'American as Cherry Pie,' Peoples Temple and Violence in America," Ibid., 121–37.

39. Ian Reader, "Imagined Persecution, Aum Shinrikyo, Millennialism, and the Legitimation of Violence," in Catherine Wessinger, ed., *Millennialism, Persecution and Violence*, 171.

40. Rebecca Moore, "'American as Cherry Pie,' Peoples Temple and Violence in America," in Catherine Wessinger, ed., *Millennialism, Persecution and Violence* 135.

41. Catherine Wessinger, "Introduction," in Catherine Wessinger, ed., *Millennialism, Persecution and Violence*, 38–39.

42. "The Top 40 Reasons to Doubt the Official Story of September 11," May 16, 2006, http://www.911truth.org/article.php?story=20041221155307646.

43. Steven Finkel, "Reciprocal Effects of Participation on Political Efficacy: A Panel Analysis," *American Journal of Political Science* Vol. 29 (1985), 289.

44. Shaun Bowler and Todd Donovan, "Democracy, Institutions and Attitudes about Citizen Influence on Government," *British Journal of Political Science*, Vol. 32, No. 2 (2002), 372–73.

45. Luke Keele, "Social Capital and the Dynamics of Trust in Government," *American Journal of Political Science*, Vol. 51, No. 2 (2007), 244.

46. Jeffrey M. Jones, "Trust in Government Remains Low," Gallup, September 18, 2008, http://www.gallup.com/poll/110458/Trust-Government-Remains-Low.aspx.

47. Frank Newport, "Trust in Legislative Branch Falls to Record-Low 36%," Gallup, September 24, 2010, http://www.gallup.com/poll/143225/Trust-Legislative-Branch-Falls-Record-Low.aspx. In the first year of the survey following his election, Barack Obama's trust rating jumped to 61 percent over George W. Bush's 42 percent in September of 2008. Jeffrey M. Jones, "Trust in Government Remains Low," Gallup, September 18, 2008, http://www.gallup.com/poll/110458/Trust-Government-Remains-Low.aspx.

48. The only branch of government to escape such a decline is the judicial branch; the most recent survey, however, suggests that it is gradually losing Americans' trust. Ibid.

49. Frank Newport, "Trust in Legislative Branch Falls to Record-Low 36%," Gallup, September 24, 2010, http://www.gallup.com/poll/143225/Trust-Legislative-Branch-Falls-Record-Low.aspx.

50. John Philpott Curran, cited in Janet Ajzenstat and Ian Gentles, *Canada's Founding Debates* (Toronto: University of Toronto Press, 2003), 126. See also Suzy Platt, ed., *Respectfully Quoted, A Dictionary of Quotations* (New York: Barnes and Noble Publishing, 1993), 200.

51. Thomas Flanagan, "The Politics of the Millennium," 173.

52. See, for example, his discussion of this term in Eric Voegelin, *Anamnesis,* Gerhart Niemeyer, trans. and ed. (Notre Dame, IN: Notre Dame Press, 1978), 170.

53. Thomas Flanagan, "The Politics of the Millennium," 173.

54. Immanuel Wallerstein, "America and the World: The Twin Towers as Metaphor," Charles R. Lawrence II Memorial Lecture, Brooklyn College, Dec. 5, 2001, Social Science Research Council, http://essays.ssrc.org/sept11/essays/wallerstein.htm.

Bibliography

Aaronovitch, David. *Voodoo Histories, The Role of the Conspiracy Theory in Shaping Modern History.* New York: Riverhead, 2010.

Abalakina-Paap, Marina, Walter G. Stephan, Traci Craig, and W. Larry Gregory. "Beliefs in Conspiracies." *Political Psychology,* Vol. 20, No. 3 (Sept. 1999): 637–647.

"Above the Law." *The Washington Post Times Herald,* April 22, 1966, A20.

"AIDS Is Man-Made—Interview with Dr. Boyd Graves." *The Final Call,* October 5, 2004. http://www.finalcall.com/artman/publish/article_1597.shtml.

Ajzenstat, Janet, and Ian Gentles. *Canada's Founding Debates.* Toronto: University of Toronto Press, 2003.

Al-Fayed, Mohamed. "Diana and Dodi, The Verdict—a Statement by Mohamed Al-Fayed." http://www.alfayed.com/dodi-and-diana/the-inquests/verdict.aspx.

Allen, Peter. "Marion Cotillard's 9/11 Conspiracy Theory." *The Daily Telegraph,* March 1, 2008. http://www.telegraph.co.uk/news/worldnews/1580414/Marion-Cotillards-911-conspiracy-theory.html.

"Amazing $20 Dollar Bill 9/11 Coincidence." http://www.allbrevard.net/_20bill/guest/.

"American Concentration Camps." http://www.apfn.org/apfn/camps.htm.

"American Girl to Marry Peer." *St. Petersburg Times,* July 16, 1921, 6.

Anti-Defamation League. "Conspiracy Theories about Jews and 9/11 Cause Dangerous Mutations in Global Anti-Semitism." September 2, 2003. http://www.adl.org/presrele/asint_13/4346_13.htm.

Anti-Defamation League. "Unravelling Anti-Semitic 9/11 Conspiracy Theories." 2003. http://www.adl.org/anti_semitism/9–11conspiracytheories.pdf.

Ardell, Donald, "Don't Buy Bottled Water." May 12, 2003, http://www.seekwellness.com/wellness/reports/2003–05–12.htm.

Arendt, Hannah. *The Human Condition.* Chicago: University of Chicago Press, 1958.

Atkins, Stephen E. *Holocaust Denial as an International Movement.* Westport, CT: Praeger, 2009.

Bagley, Gertrude. "Nearing the End of the Bourbons." *Boston Evening Transcript,* April 16, 1938, 2.

Bailyn, Bernard. *The Ideological Origins of the American Revolution.* Cambridge, MA: Harvard University Press, 1992.

Bale, Jeffrey. "Conspiracy Theories and Clandestine Politics." *Lobster* 29 (June 1995). http://www.lobster-magazine.co.uk/articles/l29consp.htm.

Barkun, Michael. *A Culture of Conspiracy, Apocalyptic Visions in Contemporary America.* Berkeley: University of California Press, 2003.

Barth, Alan. "Report on the Rampageous Right." *The New York Times Sunday Magazine,* November 26, 1961, 25, 130–31.

Bennett, David H. The *Party of Fear, From Nativist Movements to the New Right in American History.* Chapel Hill: University of North Carolina Press, 1988.

Bernstein, Carl, and Bob Woodward. "FBI Finds Nixon Aides Sabotaged Democrats," *The Washington Post,* October 10, 1972, AO1. http://www.washingtonpost.com/wpdyn/content/article/2002/06/03/AR2005111001232.html.

Billington, James. *Fire in the Minds of Men, Origins of the Revolutionary Faith.* New York: Basic Books, 1980.

Bishop, Kellene. "What Would You Do to Stop Hitler Today?" http://kellenebishop.wordpress.com/

Bjerre-Poulson, Niels. *Right Face, Organizing the American Conservative Movement, 1945–1965.* Copenhagen: Museum Tusculanum Press, 2002.

Bowler, Shaun, and Todd Donovan. "Democracy, Institutions and Attitudes about Citizen Influence on Government." *British Journal of Political Science,* Vol. 32, No. 2 (2002): 371–90.

Brasher, Barbara. "When Your Friend Is Your Enemy, American Christian Fundamentalists and Israel at the New Millennium." In Martha F. Lee, ed., *Millennial Visions: Essays on Twentieth-Century Millenarianism,* 135–47. Westport, CT: Praeger, 2000.

Brown, Dan. *The Lost Symbol.* New York: Doubleday, 2009.

Brown, Dan. *The DaVinci Code.* New York: Doubleday, 2003.

Broyles, John. *The John Birch Society: Anatomy of a Protest.* Boston: Beacon Press, 1964.

Bush, George H. W. "Address before a Joint Session of the Congress on the Cessation of the Persian Gulf Conflict." March 6, 1991. George Bush Presidential Library and Museum. http://bushlibrary.tamu.edu/research/public_papers.php?id=2767&year=1991&month=3.

Bush, George H. W. "Address before a Joint Session of the Congress on the Persian Gulf Crisis and the Federal Budget Deficit." September 11, 1990. http://bushlibrary.tamu.edu/research/public_papers.php?id=2217&year=1990&month=9.

Cannadine, David. *In Churchill's Shadow, Confronting the Past in Modern Britain.* Oxford: Oxford University Press, 2003.

Carr, E. H. *The Twenty Years' Crisis.* Introduction by Michael Cox. New York: Palgrave, 2001.

Cary, Lucian. "Recent Fiction." *The Dial,* August 16, 1914, 107.

Casanova. *Histoire de ma vie.* Paris: Brockhaus-Plon, 1960.

Centers for Disease Control and Prevention. "U.S. Public Health Service Study at Tuskegee, Tuskegee Timeline." http://www.cdc.gov/tuskegee/timeline.htm.

Churchill, Winston. "Zionism versus Bolshevism, A Struggle for the Soul of the Jewish People." *Illustrated Sunday Herald,* February 8, 1920, 5.

"Clinton: Vast Right-Wing Conspiracy is Back." Associated Press, March 13, 2007. http://www.msnbc.msn.com/id/17593375/.

Cohen, Edward S. *The Politics of Globalization in the United States.* Washington, D.C.: Georgetown University Press, 2001.

Cooper, Barry. *New Political Religions, or an Analysis of Modern Terrorism.* Columbia: University of Missouri Press, 2005.

"The Covenant of the Islamic Resistance Movement (Hamas)." August 18, 1988. http://www.mideastweb.org/hamas.htm.

Cox, Michael. "Whatever Happened to American Decline? International Relations and the New United States Hegemony." *New Political Economy,* Vol. 6, No. 3 (2001), 311–40.

Crewdson, John M. "C.I.A. Secretly Owned Insurance Complex and Invested Profits in Stock Market." *The New York Times,* April 27, 1976, 25.

Dargaville, Michael. "The Illuminati and the Galactic Federation." http://www.luis prada.com/Protected/the_illuminati_and_the_galactic_federation.htm.

"David Icke You Are a Moron." http://www.abovetopsecret.com/forum/thread 269247/pg1.

Davidson, W. Bro. Alex. "The Masonic Concept of Liberty, Freemasonry and the Enlightenment." *Pietre-Stones Review of Freemasonry.* http://www.freemasons-freemasonry.com/Davidson.html.

Davies, Norman. *Europe, A History.* London: Pimlico, 1997.

"The Da Vinci Code." May 6, 2006, http://www.rcdow.org.uk/davincicode/.

Davis, David Brion, ed. *The Fear of Conspiracy: Images of Un-American Subversion from the Revolution to the Present.* Ithaca, NY: Cornell University Press, 1971.

Dean, Jodi. *Aliens in America: Conspiracy Cultures from Outerspace to Cyberspace.* Ithaca, NY: Cornell University Press, 1998.

Dentith, Matthew. "The Simplification Hypothesis." *All Embracing, But Underwhelming.* June 22, 2006. http://all-embracing.episto.org/2006/06/22/the-simplification-hypothesis/.

Desaguliers, J. T. *The Constitutions of the Free-Masons containing the History, Charges, Regulations, &c. Of that now Ancient and Right Worshipful Fraternity. For the Use of the Lodges, London, 1723.* http://www.archive.org/stream/consti tutionsoff00andeuoft#page/n19/mode/2up.

Desborough, Brian. "Did British Intelligence Orchestrate Diana's Death?" http://www.dianaprincessofwales.net/didbritisintelligenceorchestrateprincessdianas death.htm.

Diamond, Sara. *Roads to Dominion: Right Wing Movements and Political Power in the United States.* New York: Guilford Press, 1995.

Drennen, Kyle. "CBS: Alec Baldwin 'Easy Target' for 'Conservative Junkyard Dog' Sean Hannity." *NewsBusters, Exposing and Combating Liberal Media Bias.* March 12, 2008.http://newsbusters.org/blogs/kyle-drennen/2008/05/12/cbs-alec-baldwin-easy-target-conservative-junkyard-dog-sean-hannity.

Durham, Martin. *The Christian Right: The Far Right and the Boundaries of American Conservatism.* Manchester, UK: Manchester University Press, 2000.

Durham, Martin. *Women and Fascism.* London: Routledge, 1998.

Dwight, Timothy. Sermon, cited in Vernon Stauffer, *New England and the Bavarian Illuminati.* PhD Dissertation, Columbia University, New York, 1918. Reprinted by Bibliobazaar.

Eco, Umberto. *Foucault's Pendulum.* London: Picador, 1990.

Edwards, Lee. *Conservative Revolution, The Movement That Remade America.* New York: Free Press, 1999.

Enloe, Cynthia. *Bananas, Beaches and Bases.* Berkeley: University of California Press, 1989.

Farr, Barbara Storm. *The Development and Impact of Right-Wing Politics in Britain, 1903–1932.* New York: Garland, 1987.

Faulkner, William. "Banquet Speech." The Nobel Prize. http://nobelprize.org/nobel_prizes/literature/laureates/1949/faulkner-speech.html

Fay, Sidney B. "The French Revolution." *The American Political Science Review,* Vol. 14 (1920): 732–33.

Federal Bureau of Investigation. "The F.B.I.: A Centennial History, 1908–2008." http://www.fbi.gov/fbihistorybook.htm#chapter4.

Fenster, Mark. *Conspiracy Theories, Secrecy and Power in American Culture.* Minneapolis: University of Minnesota Press, 1999.

Finkel, Steven. "Reciprocal Effects of Participation on Political Efficacy: A Panel Analysis." *American Journal of Political Science,* Vol. 29 (1985): 289–314.

Flanagan, Thomas E. "Modernity and the Millennium: From Robespierre to Radical Feminism." In Martha F. Lee, ed., *Millennial Visions: Essays on Twentieth-Century Millenarianism,* 3–16. Westport, CT: Praeger, 2000.

Flanagan, Thomas E. "The Politics of the Millennium." In Michael Barkun, ed., *Millennialism and Violence,* 164–75. London: Frank Cass, 1996.

Fling, Fred. "The French Revolution." *The American Historical Review,* Vol. 25, 714.

"Football Story." http://tribes.tribe.net/oldeschoolfootball/thread/ac4ee7da-69b7–49ce-a984–2afe5d0bc585.

Fried, Richard. *Nightmare in Red, The McCarthy Era in Perspective.* New York: Oxford University Press, 1991.

Gardell, Mattias. *In the Name of Elijah Muhammad, Louis Farrakhan and the Nation of Islam.* Durham, NC: Duke University Press, 1996.

Gill, Stephen. "The Global Organic Crisis: Paradoxes, Dangers, and Opportunities." *Monthly Review Magazine,* February 15, 2010. http://mrzine.monthlyreview. org/2010/gill150210.html#_edn6.

Gill, Stephen. "Gramsci, Modernity and Globalization." International Gramsci Society. January, 2003. http://www.internationalgramscisociety.org/resources/ online_articles/articles/gill01.shtml.

Gilman, Richard. *Behind World Revolution, The Strange Case of Nesta Webster.* Ann Arbor, MI: Insights Books, 1982.

"The Glen Beck Conspiracy Theory Generator." http://politicalhumor.about.com/ library/bl-glenn-beck-conspiracy.htm.

The Global Language Monitor. "How 9/11 Changed the Way Americans Speak." September 10, 2008. http://www.languagemonitor.com/?s = 9%2F11.

Goertzel, Ted. "Belief in Conspiracy Theories." *Political Psychology,* Vol. 15, No. 4 (1994): 731–42.

Gottlieb, Julie. *Feminine Fascism, Women in Britain's Fascist Movement.* London: I. B. Taurus, 2003.

Grant, George. *Technology and Empire: Perspectives on North America.* Toronto: House of Anansi, 1969.

Gray, Matthew. "Explaining Conspiracy Theories in Modern Arab Middle Eastern Political Discourse: Some Problems and Limitations of the Literature." *Critique: Critical Middle Eastern Studies,* Vol. 17, No. 2 (Summer 2008): 155–74.

Graves, Boyd. "The History of the Development of AIDS." http://www.boydgraves. com/timeline.

Griffin, G. Edward. *The Life and Words of Robert Welch, Founder of the John Birch Society.* Thousand Oaks, CA: American Media, 1975.

Groh, Dieter. "The Temptation of Conspiracy Theory, or: Why Do Bad Things Happen to Good People? Part I: Preliminary Draft of a Theory of Conspiracy Theories." In Carl Graumann and Serge Moscovici, eds., *Changing Conceptions of Conspiracy,* 1–13. New York: Springer-Verlag, 1987.

Gunther, Marie. "Huge Alaska Oil Reserves Go Unused." *The Spotlight.* http://www. libertylobby.org/articles/2001/20010313alaska_oil.html.

Haiikala, Sisko. "Denouncing the Enlightenment by Means of a Conspiracy Thesis, Göchhausen's Enthüllung der Weltbürgerrepublik." Translated by Pasi Ihalainen. http://www.jyu.fi/yhtfil/redescriptions/Yearbook%202000/Haikala%202000.pdf.

Hall, Manly P. *The Lost Keys of Freemasonry.* New York: Jeremy P. Tarcher, 2006.

Hargrove, Thomas. "Third of Americans Suspect 9–11 Government Conspiracy." Scripps News, August 1, 2006. http://www.scrippsnews.com/911poll.

Hersh, Seymour M. "Underground for the C.I.A. in New York: An Ex-Agent Tells of Spying on Students." *The New York Times,* December 29, 1974, 1.

"The History of Freemasons' Hall." The United Grand Lodge of England. http:// www.ugle.org.uk/ugle/the-history-of-freemasons-hall.htm.

"History of the Illuminati." http://people.virginia.edu/~sfr/enam481/groupa/illu mhist.html.

Hobbes, Thomas. *Leviathan*. Indianapolis, IN: Hackett Publishing, 1994.

Hofstadter, Richard. "The Paranoid Style in American Politics." *The Paranoid Style in American Politics, and Other Essays*. New York: Alfred A. Knopf, 1966.

Hole, Richard. "True Conspiracies, the Illuminati, and One World Government, A Conspiracy by the International Bankers, Jesuits, Illuminati and Other Groups." http://www.trueconspiracies.com/.

Holmes, Colin. *Anti-Semitism in British Society, 1876–1939*. London: Edward Arnold, 1979.

Horrock, Nicholas M. "80 Institutions Used in C.I.A. Mind Studies." *The New York Times*, August 4, 1977, 17.

Horrock, Nicholas M. "238 Break-Ins Committed by F.B.I. over 26 Years." *The New York Times*, September 26, 1975, 77.

International Committee of the Red Cross. "Protocol Additional to the Geneva Conventions of 12 August 1949, and relating to the Protection of Victims of International Armed Conflicts (Protocol I)." June 8, 1977, http://www.icrc.org/ ihl.nsf/COM/470–750042?OpenDocument.

Jackson, Camille. "Fightin' Words." Southern Poverty Law Center Intelligence Report, 15 (Fall 2004). http://www.splcenter.org/get-informed/intelligence-report/ browse-all-issues/2004/fall/fightin-words.

James, Nigel. "Militias, the Patriot movement, and the Internet: The Ideology of Conspiracism." In Jane Parish and Martin Parker, eds., *The Age of Anxiety*, 63–92. Oxford: Blackwell, 2001.

"The John Birch Society." Political Research Associates. http://www.publiceye.org/ tooclose/jbs.html.

Johnson, George. *Architects of Fear, Conspiracy Theories and Paranoia in American Politics*. Los Angeles: Jeremy Tarcher, 1983.

Jones, Jeffrey M. "Trust in Government Remains Low." Gallup, September 18, 2008. http://www.gallup.com/poll/110458/Trust-Government-Remains-Low.aspx.

Kaldor, Mary. *New and Old Wars*. 2nd ed. Palo Alto, CA: Stanford University Press, 2007.

Kaplan, Jeffrey. "The Politics of Rage, Militias and the Future of the Far Right." *The Christian Century*, June 19–26, 1996, 657–62. http://www.religion-online. org/showarticle.asp?title=226.

Kaplan, Jeffrey, ed. *The Encyclopedia of White Power, A Sourcebook on the Racist Right*. Walnut Creek, CA: Altamira Press, 2000.

Kay, Jonathan. "Black Helicopters over Nashville." *Newsweek*, February 9, 2010. http://www.newsweek.com/2010/02/08/black-helicopters-over-nashville.html.

Keele, Luke. "Social Capital and the Dynamics of Trust in Government." *American Journal of Political Science*, Vol. 51, No. 2 (2007): 791–808.

Knickerbocker, Brad. "'Ground Zero Mosque' Debate Hits the Streets of New York." *The Christian Science Monitor,* August 22, 2010. http://www.csmonitor.com/USA/2010/0822/Ground-Zero-mosque-debate-hits-the-streets-of-New-York.

"Knigge: Illuminati Weishaupt was a Jesuit in Disguise." http://troyspace2.word press.com/2008/09/16/knigge-illuminati-weishaupt-was-a-jesuit-in-disguise/.

Knight, Peter. "A Nation of Conspiracy Theorists." In Peter Knight, ed., *Conspiracy Nation: The Politics of Paranoia in Postwar America,* 1–17. New York: New York University Press, 2002.

Kraft, Joseph. "Developing a 'Gullibility Gap.'" *The Washington Post,* January 23, 1975, A23.

Krauss, Clifford. "28 Years after Kennedy's Assassination, Conspiracy Theories Refuse to Die." *The New York Times,* January 5, 1992. http://www.nytimes.com/1992/01/05/us/28-years-after-kennedy-s-assassination-conspiracy-theories-refuse-to-die.html.

Krauthammer, Charles. "A Rash of Conspiracy Theories; When Do We Dig Up Bill Casey?" *The Washington Post,* July 5, 1991. http://www.highbeam.com/doc/1P2–1073359.html.

Krebs, Valdis E. "Uncloaking Terrorist Networks." *First Monday,* Vol. 7, No. 4 (April 2002). http://firstmonday.org/htbin/cgiwrap/bin/ojs/index.php/fm/article/view/941/863.

Laqueur, Walter. *The Changing Face of Anti-Semitism, From Ancient Times to the Present Day.* Oxford: Oxford University Press, 2006.

Lee, Martha F. *Earth First! Environmental Apocalypse.* Syracuse, NY: Syracuse University Press, 1995.

Lee, Martha F., and Herbert Simms. "American Millenarianism and Violence: Origins and Expressions." *Journal for the Study of Radicalism,* Vol. 2, No. 2 (2008): 107–27.

Le Forestier, René. *Les Illuminés de Bavière et la franc-maçonnerie allemande.* Geneva: Slatkine-Megariotis Reprints, 1974.

Levy, Joel. *The Little Book of Conspiracies.* London: Key Porter Books, 2006.

Lindemann, Albert S. *Anti-Semitism before the Holocaust.* Harlow, England: Longman, 2000.

Locke, John. *Second Treatise on Government.* Indianapolis, IN: Hackett, 1980.

Loose Change Fact Sheet. *Loose Change* 9/11, An American Coup. http://www.loosechange911.com/about/faq/.

"Lord Queensborough [*sic*] Married to Edith Starr Miller." *Pittsburgh Gazette-Times,* July 20, 1921, 2.

Macdonald, Andrew [William Pierce]. *The Turner Diaries.* http://www.jrbookson line.com/PDF_Books/TurnerDiaries.pdf.

Manning, Martin J., and Herbert Romerstein. *Historical Dictionary of American Propaganda.* Westport, CT: Greenwood Publishing, 2004.

Marek, Michael. "The X-Files Timeline." http://www.themareks.com/xf/index. html.

Marquis, Don. "Former Illuminist Witch Reveals Strong Witchcraft Ties to Free- masonry." http://letsrollforums.com/kurt-cobain-mind-control-17443p30.html ?s=16e58c34074dd73bcfc5accf80a25927&amp.

Marr, Andrew. *A History of Modern Britain.* London: MacMillan, 2007.

"Masonic Membership Statistics." The Masonic Service Association. http://www. msana.com/msastats.asp.

McConnachie, James, and Robin Tudge. *The Rough Guide to Conspiracy Theories.* London: Penguin Books, 2005.

Mercola, Joseph. "Airport Scanners: Radiation Is *Not* the Only Health Hazard." *The Huffington Post,* December 15, 2010. http://www.huffingtonpost.com/dr- mercola/airport-scanners-how-much-radiation-_b_793071.html.

Miller, Edith Starr. *Common Sense in the Kitchen.* New York: Brentino's, 1918.

Miller, Edith Starr [Lady Queenborough]. *Occult Theocrasy.* Reprint of the 1933 edition. Palmdale, CA: Christian Book Club of America, 1976.

Millman, Joyce. "'The X-Files' Finds the Truth: Its Time Is Past." *The New York Times,* May 19, 2002. http://www.nytimes.com/2002/05/19/arts/television/19MILL. html?scp=1&sq=%22is%20the%20truth%20out%20there%22&st=cse.

Modelski, George. "Long Cycles in Global Politics." https://faculty.washington.edu/ modelski/LCGPeolss.htm.

Moore, Rebecca. " 'American as Cherry Pie,' Peoples Temple and Violence in America." In Catherine Wessinger, ed., *Millennialism, Persecution and Violence,* 121–37. Syracuse, NY: Syracuse University Press, 2000.

Moscovici, Serge. "The Conspiracy Mentality." In Carl Graumann and Serge Mos- covici, eds., *Changing Conceptions of Conspiracy,* 151–68. London: Springer- Verlag, 1987.

"A Mosque at Ground Zero, Not Here, Not Ever." *The Daily Mail Online,* Au- gust 23, 2010. http://synonblog.dailymail.co.uk/2010/08/a-mosque-at-ground- zero-not-here-not-ever.html.

"Mrs. Nesta Webster, Studies in French History." Obituary. *The Times,* May 18, 1960, 17.

Newport, Frank. "Trust in Legislative Branch Falls to Record-Low 36%." Gallup, Sep- tember 24, 2010. http://www.gallup.com/poll/143225/Trust-Legislative-Branch- Falls-Record-Low.aspx.

Next Up: Who Killed Huey?" *Chicago Sun-Times.* http://www.highbeam.com/ doc/1P2–4060854.html.

Niebuhr, Gustav. "Pat Robertston Says He Intended No Anti-Semitism in Book He Wrote Four Years Ago." *The New York Times,* March 4, 1995. http://www.ny times.com/1995/03/04/us/pat-robertston-says-he-intended-no-anti-semitism- in-book-he-wrote-four-years-ago.html?scp=9&sq=.

"911Truth.org: An Overview." August 26, 2004. http://www.911truth.org/article.ph
p?story=20061014120445472#mission.

Oliver, Revilo P. "A Centennial You Should Notice." *The Liberty Bell,* December
1988. http://www.revilo-oliver.com/rpo/Centennial.html.

Oliver, Revilo P. "Conspiracy or Degeneracy." Speech to the New England Rally
for God, Family, and Country." Boston, 1966. http://www.revilo-oliver.com/
news/1966/07/conspiracy-or-degeneracy/.

Oliver, Revilo P. "Contemporary Journalists." *The Liberty Bell,* February 1985.
http://www.revilo-oliver.com/rpo/Contemporary_Journalists.html.

Oliver, Revilo. "Marxmanship in Dallas [Part II]." American *Opinion,* Vol. 7,
No. 3 (March 1964): 65–78. http://www.kenrahn.com/jfk/the_critics/oliver/
marxmanship_in_dallas_ii.html.

Olmsted, Kathryn S. *Real Enemies, Conspiracy Theories and American Democracy,
World War 1 to 9/11.* Oxford: Oxford University Press, 2009.

Oxford English Dictionary Online. http://dictionary.oed.com/cgi/entry/50048058?
single=1&query_type=word&queryword=conspire&first=1&max_to_
show=10.

"PAPERBACK BEST SELLERS: January 20, 1991—New York Times." *The New York
Times.* http://www.highbeam.com/doc/1S1–9199101200004091.html.

Parkman, Francis. *Montcalm and Wolfe.* Vol. 2. Boston: Little, Brown, and Company, 1884.

Patterson, James T. *Grand Expectations: the United States, 1945–74.* Oxford: Oxford
University Press, 1997.

Pauli, Michelle. "Dan Brown's The Lost Symbol Breaks Records for First Week
Sales." *The Guardian,* September 22, 2009. http://www.guardian.co.uk/books/
2009/sep/22/dan-brown-lost-symbol-record-sales.

"Paul McCartney Really Is Dead." http://www.paulreallyisdead.com/.

Penre, Wes. "The Secret Order of the Illuminati, A Brief History of the Shadow
Government." *The Illuminati News,* November 12, 1998, updated September 26,
2009. http://www.illuminati-news.com/moriah.htm#2.

Peterson, Daneen. "About the NAU—What you Don't Know CAN Hurt You."
Speech. Washington, D.C., June 15, 2007. http://www.stopthenorthamerican
union.com/WhatYouDontKnow.html.

Pew Research Center for People and the Press. "Growing Number of Americans Say
Obama is a Muslim." August 19, 2010. http://people-press.org/report/645/.

Pipes, Daniel. *Conspiracy, How the Paranoid Style Flourishes and Where it Comes
From.* New York: Free Press, 1997.

Platt, Suzy, ed. *Respectfully Quoted, A Dictionary of Quotations.* New York: Barnes
and Noble, 1993.

Pratt, Ray. "Theorizing Conspiracy." *Theory and Society,* Vol. 32, No. 2 (April 2003):
255–71.

"President Zachary Taylor Just Plain Died in Office." *Albany Times Union,* June 27, 1991. http://www.highbeam.com/doc/1G1–156232096.html.

Program on International Policy Attitudes, University of Maryland. "International Poll: No Consensus on Who was Behind 9/11," http://www.worldpublicopinion. org/pipa/articles/international_security_bt/535.php?nid=&id=&pnt=535.

Ratzinger, Cardinal Joseph. "Declaration on Masonic Associations." Congregation for the Doctrine of the Faith, November 26, 1983. http://www.vati can.va/roman_curia/congregations/cfaith/documents/rc_con_cfaith_doc_ 19831126_declaration-masonic_en.html.

Reader, Ian. "Imagined Persecution, Aum Shinrikyo, Millennialism, and the Legitimation of Violence." In Catherine Wessinger, ed., *Millennialism, Persecution and Violence,* 158–84. Syracuse, NY: Syracuse University Press, 2000.

"Reflections a Year after Declaration of Congregation for the Doctrine of the Faith, Irreconcilability between Christian Faith and Freemasonry." *L'Osservatore Romano,* March 11, 1985. http://www.vatican.va/roman_curia/congregations/ cfaith/documents/rc_con_cfaith_doc_19850223_declarationmasonic_ articolo_en.html.

Reich, Robert B. *The Work of Nations.* Toronto: Random House, 1992.

Roberts, Adam. "Lives and Statistics: Are 90% of War Victims Civilians?" *Survival,* Vol. 52, No. 3 (2010): 115–36.

Roberts, J. M. *The Mythology of the Secret Societies.* London: Secker and Warburg, 1972.

Robertson, Pat. *The New World Order.* Dallas, TX: Word Publishing, 1991.

Robison, John. *Proofs of a Conspiracy against All of the Religions and Governments of Europe.* Reprint. Whitefish, MT: Kessinger, 2003.

Ronson, Jon. "Conspirators." *The Guardian,* May 5, 2001. http://www.guardian. co.uk/world/2001/may/05/mcveigh.usa.

Rosecrance, Richard. "Long Cycle Theory in International Relations." *International Organization.* Vol. 41, No. 2 (1987): 283–301.

Rumsfeld, Donald. "Web Site OPSEC Discrepancies." United States Government Department of Defense, January 14, 2003. http://www.defense.gov/webmasters/ policy/rumsfeld_memo_to_DOD_webmasters.html.

Ruotsila, Markku. "Mrs. Webster's Religion: Conspiracist Extremism on the Christian Far Right," *Patterns of Prejudice,* Vol. 38, No. 2, 107–26.

"Russia: World's Leader in State Sponsored Terrorism!!!" *Newswatch Magazine,* July 1, 2002. http://newswatchmagazine.org/julyaug02/julyaug02.htm.

"Satanic Voices." Islamic Party of Britain, March 26, 2003. http://www.islamicparty. com/satvoices/acknowledgements.htm.

"Satellite Network Recycles The Protocols of the Elders of Zion." The Anti-Defamation League, January 9, 2004. http://www.adl.org/special_reports/ protocols/protocols_recycled.asp.

"Secret Kennedy Extraterrestrial Briefing Strengthens UFO Assassination Theories." *We Must Know,* June 29, 2010. http://wemustknow.net/2010/06/secret-kennedy-extraterrestrial-briefing-strengthens-ufo-assassination-theories/.

Select Committee to Study Governmental Operations with Respect to Intelligence Activities, United States Senate. "Intelligence Activities and the Rights of Americans." http://www.icdc.com/~paulwolf/cointelpro/churchfinalreportIIb.htm.

"The Sheep Track." *The Bookman* (1914), 94–95.

"The Sheep Track," *The New York Times,* August 16, 1914, 346.

"The Sheep Track." *The New York Times,* March 16, 1919, 137.

"The Sheep Track." *The Spectator,* April 11, 1913, 617.

"SMOKING GUN PROOF THAT ILLUMINATI PLAN TO ATTACK ON 9/11 AND BEYOND WAS WELL KNOWN AS FAR BACK AS 1995! Part 1—Future Cataclysmic Events Accurately Foretold In 1995 Illuminati Card Game—9/11 Attack Foreseen." http://www.cuttingedge.org/news/n1753.cfm.

Sovereign Great Priory of Canada. "Chivalry and Freemasonry." 2003. http://www.knightstemplar.ca/history/index.htm.

Spier, Howard. "'Zionists and Freemasons' in Soviet Propaganda." *Patterns of Prejudice,* Vol. 13, No. 1 (1979): 1–5.

Sproull, Lee, and Sara Kiesler. *Connections, New Ways of Working in the Networked Organization.* Boston: MIT Press, 1992.

Stauffer, Vernon. *New England and the Bavarian Illuminati.* PhD Dissertation, Columbia University, New York, 1918. Reprinted by Bibliobazaar.

Stenzel, James. "Dumping Goy Politics." *The Jew Watch.* http://www.jewwatch.com/jew-worldconspiracies-illuminati.html.

Stone, Barbara. "The John Birch Society: A Profile." *The Journal of Politics,* Vol. 36, No. 1 (Feb. 1974): 184–97.

Strozier, Charles B., and Katharine Boyd. "The Psychology of Apocalypticism." *The Journal of Psychohistory,* Vol. 37, No. 4 (Spring 2010): 276–95.

Swami, Viren, Tomas Chamorro-Premuzic, and Adrian Furnham. "Unanswered Questions: A Preliminary Investigation of Personality and Individual Difference Predictors of 9/11 Conspiracist Beliefs." *Applied Cognitive Psychology* (May 2009) (DOI: 10.1002/acp.1583). http://www3.interscience.wiley.com/journal/122386128/abstract.

Sweet, Joanna, and Martha F. Lee. "Christian Exodus: A Modern American Millenarian Movement." *Journal for the Study of Radicalism,* Vol. 4, No. 1 (2010): 1–23.

Talmon, Jacob L. *The Origins of Totalitarian Democracy.* New York: Praeger, 1960.

Talmon, Yonina. "Millenarism" *Encyclopedia of the Social Sciences,* Vol. 10, 349–62. New York: MacMillan, 1968.

Taylor, Alan. "Two Biographies." *The Manchester Guardian,* Nov. 13, 1936, 7.

Team Infinity. "Oklahoma City Bombing Questions Demand an Answer." http://www.stopcovertwar.com/McVeigh.html.

"Thunder against the Right." *Time,* November 24, 1961.

Thurlow, Richard. "The Powers of Darkness, Conspiracy Belief and Political Strategy." *Patterns of Prejudice,* Vol. 12, No. 6 (Nov.-Dec. 1978): 1–12.

"The Top 40 Reasons to Doubt the Official Story of September 11." May 16, 2006. http://911truth.org/article.php?story=20041221155307646.

Travis, Shannon. "CNN Poll: Quarter Doubt Obama Was Born in US." August 4, 2010. http://politicalticker.blogs.cnn.com/2010/08/04/cnn-poll-quarter-doubt-president-was-born-in-u-s/.

"Under Fire, Obama Clarifies Support for Ground Zero Mosque." August 14, 2010. http://www.foxnews.com/politics/2010/08/14/obamas-support-ground-zero-mosque-draws.

United States Department of Justice. Federal Bureau of Investigation. "Terrorism, 2002–2005." http://www.fbi.gov/stats-services/publications/terrorism-2002–2005/terror02_05.

United States Department of State. "The 4,000 Jews Rumor." April 28, 2009. http://www.america.gov/st/webchatenglish/2009/April/20090430132244atlahtnevel4.020327e-02.html.

Van Impe, Jack, and Rexella Van Impe. "Final World Government, When, Now?" http://www.jvim.org/pt/2004/2004SeptOct.pdf.

Voegelin, Eric. *Anamnesis.* Gerhart Niemeyer, trans. and ed. Notre Dame, IN: Notre Dame Press, 1978.

Wallace, Anthony. "Revitalization Movements." *American Anthropologist,* Vol. 58 (1956): 264–81.

Wallerstein, Immanuel. "America and the World: The Twin Towers as Metaphor." Charles R. Lawrence II Memorial Lecture, Brooklyn College. Dec. 5, 2001. Social Science Research Council. http://essays.ssrc.org/sept11/essays/wallerstein.htm.

Wallerstein, Immanuel. *The Politics of the World Economy, Essays by Immanuel Wallerstein.* Cambridge: Cambridge University Press, 1984.

Waters, Anita. "Conspiracy Theories as Ethnosociologies: Explanation and Intention in African American Political Culture." *Journal of Black Studies,* Vol. 28, No. 1 (1997): 112–25.

Watson, Paul Joseph. "Martin Sheen Questions Official 9/11 Story." October 29, 2007. http://www.prisonplanet.com/articles/october2007/291007_sheen_questions.htm.

Watt, Alan. *Transcript of the Dr. Bill Deagle Show.* June 11, 2007. http://www.alanwattsentientsentinel.eu/english/transcripts/Alan_Watt_on_BillDeagleShow_June112007.html.

Webster, Nesta. *Britain's Call to Arms, An Appeal to Our Women.* London: Hugh Rees, 1914.

Webster, Nesta. *The French Revolution, A Study in Democracy*. London: Constable, 1926.

Webster, Nesta. *Germany and England*. London: Boswell, 1938.

Webster, Nesta. "Illuminism and the World Revolution." *The Nineteenth Century and After*. Vol. 88 (July–December 1920): 97–99.

Webster, Nesta. "Marie Antoinette, A Slandered Queen." *The Nineteenth Century and After*. Vol. 1021(1937): 372–82.

Webster, Nesta. "Mrs. Nesta H. Webster on Fascism." *The British Lion* (January 7, 1927): 7.

Webster, Nesta. *The Past History of the World Revolution*. Lecture delivered at the Royal Artillery Institution, Woolwich, England. Tuesday, Nov. 30, 1920. Royal Artillery Institution Printing House, 1921.

Webster, Nesta. "The Patriots' Inquiry Centre." *The Patriot*, Vol. 12, No. 229 (October 20, 1927): 382.

Webster, Nesta. "The Progress of World Revolution." *The Patriot*, Vol. 9, No. 191 (October 1, 1925): 457–458.

Webster, Nesta. *Secret Societies and Subversive Movements*. London: Boswell, 1924.

Webster, Nesta [Julian Sterne]. *The Secret of the Zodiac*. London: Boswell, 1933.

Webster, Nesta. *The Sheep Track*. London: John Murray, 1924.

Webster, Nesta. *Spacious Days*. London: Hutchinson and Company, 1950.

Webster, Nesta. "Where Are We Going? Part 1, Socialist Dreams." *The Patriot*, Vol. 45, No. 1300 (January 9, 1947): 19–20, 72.

Webster, Nesta. "Women and Civilisation." *The Nineteenth Century and After*. Vol. 88, No. 525 (November 1920): 741–59.

Webster, Nesta. *World Revolution, The Plot against Civilization*. London: Constable and Company, 1921.

Weimann, Gabriel. "How Modern Terrorism Uses the Internet." United States Institute of Peace. Special Report 116, March 2004. http://www.usip.org/files/re sources/sr116.pdf.

Welch, Robert. *The Blue Book of the John Birch Society*. Appleton, WI: Western Islands Publishers, 2000.

Wessinger, Catherine, ed. *Millennialism, Persecution and Violence*. Syracuse, NY: Syracuse University Press, 2000.

Westin, Alan F. "The John Birch Society: 'Radical Right' and 'Extreme Left' in the Political Context of Post World War Two (1962)." In Daniel Bell, ed., *The Radical Right*, 3rd ed., 239–68, New Brunswick, NJ: Transaction Publishers, 2001.

Willis, Oliver. "Liberal Elitism? No. Some People are, Sadly, Stupid." *The Huffington Post*, August 28, 2010. http://www.huffingtonpost.com/oliver-willis/liberal-elitism-no-some-p_b_356218.html.

Winrod, Gerald. *The Truth about the Protocols*. http://www.biblebelievers.org.au/truth.htm.

Wolfson, Jill. "The World According to Mae." *The San Jose Mercury News,* March 28, 1982. http://www.maebrussell.com/Mae%20Brussell%20Articles/World%20 According%20To%20Mae.html.

Wolfstieg, August W. *Bibliographie der FreimaurerischenLiteratur.* Leipzig: Verein Deutscher Freimaurer, 1911.

Woods, Katherine. "Marie Antoinette and Louis XVI Before the Revolution." *The New York Times Book Review,* January 16, 1938, 9.

"The World Trade Center, September 11, 2001." The Revelation. http://www.the forbiddenknowledge.com/wtc/index02.htm.

Young, Robert. "Fundamentalism and Terrorism." In Jerry S. Piven, Paul Ziolo, and Henry W. Lawton, eds., *Terror and Apocalypse: Psychological Undercurrents of History,* Vol. 2, 205–43. Lincoln, NE: IUniverse, 2002.

Index

About the Author

MARTHA F. LEE is Professor of Political Science at the University of Windsor, Ontario, Canada. Her research specialization is millenarianism, and her previous works focus on the links between religious and political beliefs. They include *The Nation of Islam, An American Millenarian Movement*, and *Earth First! Environmental Apocalypse*. She is also the editor of *Millennial Visions*, published by Praeger in 2000.